KALEIDOSCOPE
ARTISTRY

COZY BAKER

C&T PUBLISHING

Editor: Cyndy Lyle Rymer
Copyeditors: Lucy Grijalva and Stacy Chamness
Design Director/Book Design: Christina D. Jarumay
Cover Design: Christina D. Jarumay
Graphic Illustrations: Jeff Carillo
Production Assistants: Jeff Carillo, Kristy A. Konitzer, Kirstie L. McCormick,
and Stephanie Muir

Front cover (clockwise from top): *Little Luni* image by Ken and Dore
Wilhoite, photo by Adam Peiperl; *Bali Hai* image by Luc and Sallie Durette,
photo by Tom Ferguson; *Gigantic Planet* by Debbie and David Rosenfeldt;
Universe 2000 image by Yuriko and Mitsuru Yoda; *Eclipse* image by Luc
and Sallie Durette, photo by Tom Ferguson; *Poseidon* (bottom) by Charles
Karadimos and James Lane Casey; *Cresere* by Glenn Straub, photo by
Gary Landsman; Image by Peggy and Steve Kittelson

Back cover (left to right): Marble scope by Henry Bergeson; *Growing
Taller* by Koji Yamami; *Parlor* scope by Bob McWilliam; *Sir Toby* by
Susan and Marc Lundgren-Tickle; *Japanese Beauty* by Yuriko and
Mitsuru Yoda; *Diamonds* image by Bob and Grace Ade; Sphere image
by Koji Yamami; *Tapestry Unfolds* image by Peggy and Steve Kittelson

Cover jacket flaps: *Slow Yo-Yo* image by Tom and Carol Paretti, photo
by Melani Weber; *Universe 2000* image by Yuriko and Mitsuru Yoda

Legal page (top to bottom): First and third images from scopes by
Luc and Sallie Durette, photos by Tom Ferguson; *On Eagle's Wings*
by Jocelyn Teh and Robert Cook; *American Freedom* image by Ken
and Dore Wilhoite, photo by Adam Peiperl

Contents (clockwise): *Daisy* image by Peggy and Steve Kittelson; *Little
Luni* image by Ken and Dore Wilhoite, photo by Adam Peiperl; *Tapestry
Unfolds* image by Peggy and Steve Kittelson; *Summer Evening* and
Spring Morning by Bob and Sue Rioux, photo by Chris Smith; *Bali Hai*
image by Luc and Sallie Durette, photo by Tom Ferguson; (center)
Eclipse image by Luc and Sallie Durette, photo by Tom Ferguson

Photographs of scopes by the individual artist (except as noted otherwise).

Library of Congress Cataloging-in-Publication Data
Baker, Cozy
    Kaleidoscope artistry / Cozy Baker.
        p. cm.
Includes index.
    ISBN 1-57120-135-1
    1. Kaleidoscopes. I. Title.
    QC373.K3 B343 2001
    688.7'2--dc21
                                            2001005346

Published by C&T Publishing, Inc.
P.O. Box 1456
Lafayette, California 94549

Printed in China
10 9 8 7 6 5 4 3 2 1

Dedicated to every caring member of the Brewster Society, and in particular, to each artist who is inspired to create his or her own variation of the kaleidoscope. This embodies the heart as well as art, and imparting the kaleidoscope's joy and beauty enriches the experience of life.

Tapestry Unfolds image from a scope by Peggy & Steve Kittelson

The kaleidoscope is like a crystal cave—all its magic is in eclipse until you take a peek. Then the magic unfolds so simply that you don't have to apply any effort, nor do you have to see what others see. In fact, it is just for you to see and read into it whatever you feel.

CONTENTS

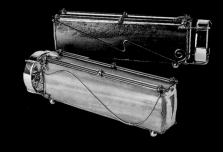

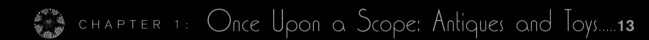

Star Angels image by David Sugich

The Kaleidoscope: A Sacred Connection

A new dawn is always breaking inside a kaleido-scope. There are some who experience a sacred connection as they view the kaleidoscope through the inner mirror of their soul. They see each image as a link to the Divine Mind and hear God's voice in the silent language of color. Whether it is a few moments of clarity or a realization of oneness, they inter-pret the unfolding mandalas as messages of love and beauty; feeling, more than seeing, the radiance within. "Listening" with an open heart enables one to discover that each kaleidoscope is a little world unto itself where one can:

hear silent music

feel wondrous harmony

count the interlacing stars

find peace and calm

experience oneness

keep dreaming dreams

realize heart swells of rapture

perceive glistening dewdrops or snow crystals

reflect on beauty repeating itself over and over again

know that for each ending there is a new beginning

Remaining focused on the image can influence one's moods and sensibilities. The ever-evolving resolution of perfect order and symmetry created from random, even chaotic, disarray is the kaleidoscope's indelible promise of hope. There is nothing sordid, only loveliness. No destruction, only rearrangement. Each new image is the re-weaving of an earlier web as the new constantly emerges from the old. The sacred connection is not just a "New Age" concept. The following excerpts are from an article originally published in 1851.

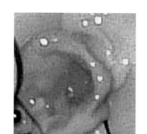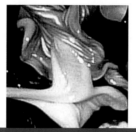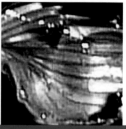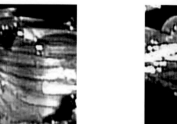

Meditation on the Wonders of the Kaleidoscope

I took up [says the Rev. Leigh Richmond] my kaleidoscope; and, as I viewed with delight the extraordinary succession of beautiful images which it presented to my sight, I was struck—1. With the singular phenomenon of perfect order being invariably and constantly produced out of perfect disorder—so that, as by magical influence, confusion and irregularity seemed to become the prolific parents of symmetry and beauty. 2. It occurred to me that the universality of its adoption would imperceptibly lead to the cultivation of the principles of taste, elegance, and beauty, through the whole of the present and following generations; and that from the philosopher and artist down to the poorest child in the community. 3. I admired the effects produced by new and varied combinations of colours, as well as forms. 4. I saw a vast accession to the sources of invention, in its application to the elegant arts and manufacturers, and the consequent growth of a more polished and highly cultivated state of habits, manners, and refinement in both. 5. I mused with delight on the powers and effects of geometrical arrangement and combination, so easily exhibited to the eye, and so characteristic of the optical principle on which the instrument is constructed. 6. I was struck with the idea of infinite variety more strikingly demonstrated to the eye than by any former experiment. Here the sublime mingles with the beautiful. 7. I perceived a kind of visible music. The combination of form and colour produced harmony—their succession, melody: thus, what an organ or pianoforte is to the ear, the kaleidoscope is to the eye. I was delighted with this analogy between the senses, as exercised in this interesting experiment.

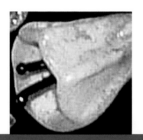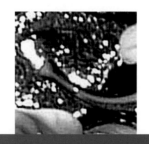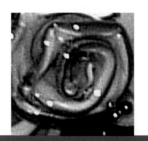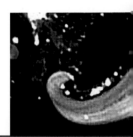

I took up my kaleidoscope again, and was lost in the contemplation of its use and beauties, to think— 1. Here I seem to see, on the one hand, the ruin and disorder of human nature, and, on the other, the marvelous influence of grace in producing out of these materials—order, beauty, and restoration. 2. My instrument I compared to a telescope-glass, which faith and hope had put into my hand; I saw through one end of the tube the world, and our life in it, a scene of confusion and tribulation, strange revolutions, and mysterious complexities. Through the other I beheld promised delights, heavenly realities, beauty for ashes, and the wilderness blooming like a rose. I took the hint, and saw reasons for resignation, contentment, and patient waiting for the glory that shall be revealed. 3. I observed, as I gently turned my instrument round, how quickly the pleasures of sense vanished. The phantom which delighted me but a moment before was gone—forever gone— irrecoverably lost! Let me not, then, said I, set my heart on that which so quickly taketh wing and fleeith away. Such is the world and its delights. 4. But, again as I looked, new beauties constantly succeeded those which had passed away. 5. When I look at my little fragments of glass and stones, and observe how, from such apparently despicable materials, such beauty and symmetry arise, I learn not to despise the day of small things, and to count nothing unworthy of my notice. (*Hogg's Instructor*, Vol. VI, new series (1851), Edinburgh.)

*Excerpt submitted by scope collector Vince Cianfichi

Flame-worked glass pieces by Peggy and Steve Kittelson used in their kaleidoscope cells

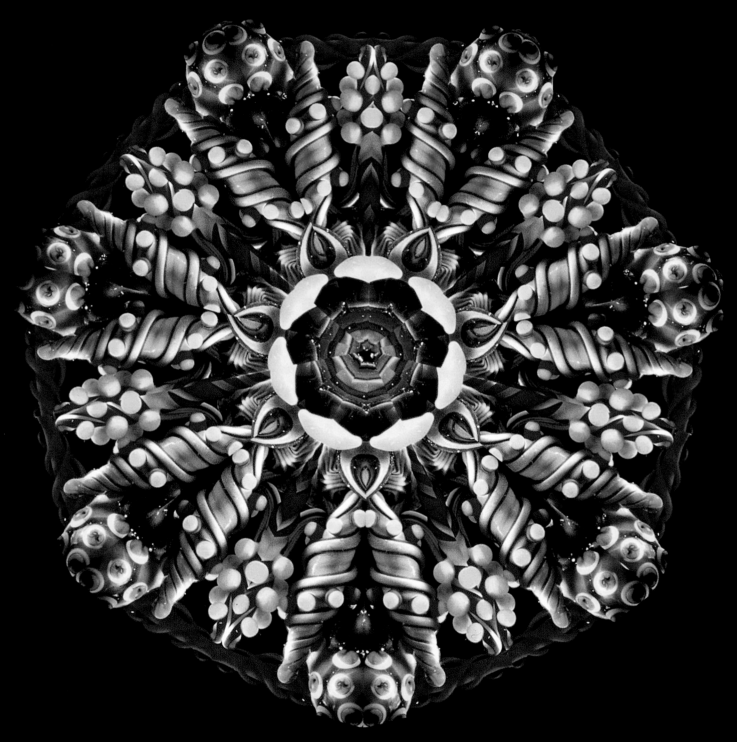

Image through **Bali Hai** by Luc and Sallie Durette. Photo by Tom Ferguson

C H A P T E R

Once Upon a Scope: Antiques and Toys

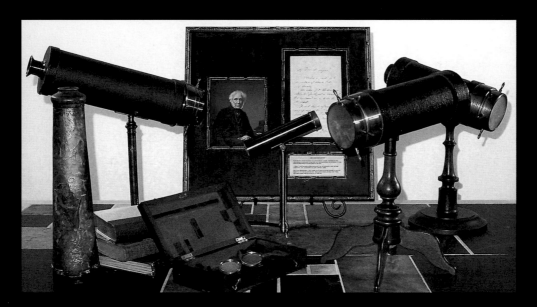

Antique kaleidoscopes from the collection of Kevin Kohler

Each pattern, beautiful in its balance, yet over and over something new.
Each image, completing a cycle, yet ever and ever something beyond.

W. Leigh Newton kaleidoscope. Photo courtesy of Sotheby's

Antique scopes from the collection of Cozy Baker

Old toy scopes. Photo by Lisa Masson

From the collection of Cozy Baker

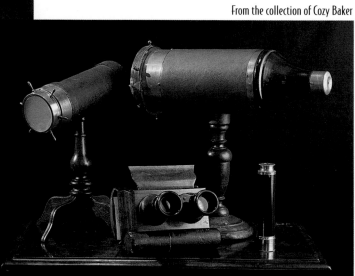

Kaleidoscopes are portals of remembrance that open onto the familiar, yet unexpected. Allowing the eye to marvel, the mind to explore, and the heart to leap, these mirrored tubes of magic have developed into a significant new art form. Since its invention by Sir David Brewster in 1816, the kaleidoscope has fulfilled a variety of functions. Universal in appeal and spanning all age groups, it has served as a toy for children, parlor entertainment for adults, and a design palette for artists, jewelers, architects, and all those involved in the ornamental arts.

Since its nineteenth-century origin, the kaleidoscope has developed by light-years in design, optics, and sheer beauty. While its name alone promises the magic of Aladdin's lamp or Cinderella's fairy godmother, it takes more than a magic lamp or wand to transform yesterday's "Victorian videos" into modern "space-age spectaculars." First and foremost it takes the hands and heart of a dedicated artist. Indeed, the artist is the very heart of the kaleidoscope, and kaleidoscope artists are what scopes are all about—an aurora borealis of color.

The artists introduced in this book are limited to those who are creating kaleidoscopes as the twenty-first century gets under way. This means that many of the familiar names of artists who have played an important role in the kaleidoscope renaissance, if they are no longer designing and producing scopes, are not included.

Although the artists are nearly as diverse in their backgrounds, ambitions, and pursuits as the instrument's myriad images, they all feel intuitively drawn to create their own interpretation of the kaleidoscope. Each artist strives to create some original concept or unique workmanship to distinguish his or her scopes from those of any other. Michelangelo would have loved kaleidoscopes. He once wrote, "Gazing on beautiful things acts on my soul, which thirsts for heavenly light."

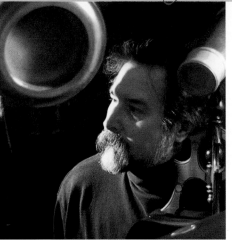

A fascination with old scientific instruments, as well as the architecture and furniture of the late nineteenth century, inspires the style of Wiley Jobe's kaleidoscopes. He uses his favorite and most familiar medium, wood, and concentrates on Brewster's most sophisticated and difficult mirror system, the polyangular. Very few artists use this hinged system that allows the mirrors to open and close, resulting in images that contain from two to twenty reflected points.

Images created by a polyangular mirror system

Wiley began making kaleidoscopes in the fall of 1987 to amuse a young friend. That Sunday afternoon project soon got out of control and catapulted into a full "part-time" career. At that point Wiley had never heard of Sir David Brewster and was blissfully unaware that a kaleidoscope renaissance was already underway without him. In retrospect, he is happy that he was able to discover kaleidoscopes at his own pace and without the benefit of seeing the work of other artists. That made it easier to develop his special niche in the scope world.

Wiley is one kaleidoscope artist whose personality and character traits are in direct contrast to the work he produces. His dry wit and imaginative sense of humor pervade everything he comes in contact with, even though he is quixotic one day and pragmatic the next. His work, however, is consistent and serious.

When not building kaleidoscopes, Wiley enjoys playing bass and piano with an aging blues band, fishing, astronomy, and flying kites and airplanes. His goal is to sell enough scopes to buy an old biplane and go barnstorming around the country, giving free plane rides, and then retire to a small island in the South Pacific. "Well," he muses, "what kind of an artist would I be if I wasn't a dreamer?"

Rumford Duo

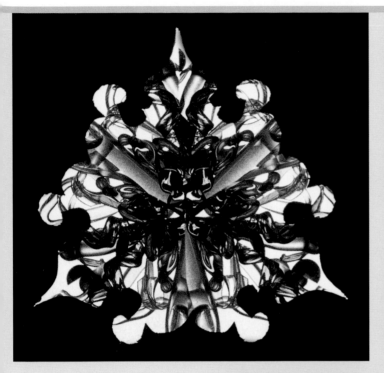

Reverie

Reproduction of working-tool
based on Brewster's patent

Triad

Carolyn Bennett

While the objective of most contemporary kaleidoscope artists is to create great ornamental and sculptural scopes, Carolyn Bennett is aware of the need for quality scopes for children as well. Her fascination with kaleidoscopes began when she was only nine years old, and has remained strong ever since. She made her first kaleidoscope from instructions in an old encyclopedia, and decided then to write a book that would make it easier for children to understand the magic of scopes. *The Kids' Book of Kaleidoscopes* (complete with a kit) is in its fifth printing at Workman Publishing.

One of the first to recognize kaleidoscopes as a valid art form, Carolyn quit teaching school to become a fulltime scope artist. That was quite a brave commitment in 1978, but one she has never had cause to regret. As an artist she uses the scope tube as her palette, and approaches the image as if it were a painting, combining colors and shapes that create a metamorphosis of enticing patterns. Her goal has always been to create high-quality scopes that are intriguing on the outside with beauty on the inside that makes you catch your breath. To achieve that, yet keep it affordable, Carolyn chose to work mainly with acrylic, elevating that medium to new standards of excellence.

Special one-of-a-kind scopes made from wedding invitations and other personal celebrations, as well as customized kaleidoscopes for individuals, museums, and corporations, are an important part of the high-volume production at C. Bennett Scopes. The inventory is varied, and to date nearly a thousand different models, including a patented camera lens ("Scopelens"), have been designed and produced by this prolific artist.

Respected and admired by her peers not only for her remarkable talent, but also for her friendly and helpful attitude, Carolyn gives generously and lovingly to the entire kaleidoscope community. While she enjoys success in every aspect of the planning and engineering that goes into creating each new scope, Carolyn admits that her chief satisfaction and happiness today comes from just being a mom!

Image of Carolyn's daughter Ana through Scopelens

Image through a three-mirror system

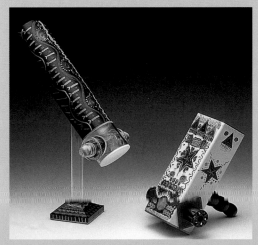

Odylic IV and **Slidoscope**. Photo by P. Groesbeck

Personalized Bennett scopes. Photo by Gary Landsman

Quadra Photo by P. Groesbeck

Parlor Cone image by Charles Karadimos

Classic Object-Cell Scopes

Poseidon, a Charles Karadimos and James Lane Casey collaboration. Photo by Charles Karadimos

One can almost imagine Aristotle gazing into a kaleidoscope when he declared, "The chief forms of beauty are order and symmetry and definiteness," or Plato, when he uttered the words, "Beauty absolute, separate, simple, and everlasting."

Lamp-worked pieces for **Dream Drops** by Sherry Moser

*S*ir David Brewster's original kaleidoscope was constructed with an interchangeable object cell (or chamber) filled with simple pieces of colored glass. Although a great many different kinds of objective endpieces have been employed through the years, kaleidoscopes using cells (filled with objects to be viewed) outnumber all other types being produced at the beginning of the twenty-first century. And for good reason—they provide images with the greatest variety and diversity.

There are numerous kinds of object cells, and each one provides its own unique pattern variance. In addition to a clear background, the cell can have a black backdrop, or one that is colored or etched. It can also be side-lit, where the light enters through the sides of the cell instead of the end. Some cells are filled with dry tumbling pieces, others are liquid-filled with floating pieces, and there is at least one that combines both a dry and a liquid cell.

Another popular type of object cell is left empty for the collector to fill with his own trinkets and treasures. Cells can be recessed, or attached to the end of the scope. A few are equipped with filters that polarize the light. No doubt by the time this book went to press there was something new in object cells.

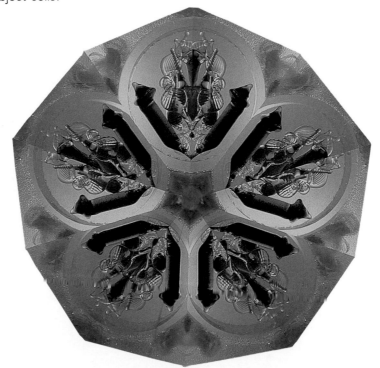

Reaching for the Stars image by Sherry Moser

Charles Karadimos

If kaleidoscope connoisseurs were asked to compile a list of the top ten artists, it is almost certain the name Charles Karadimos would be on every list. Whether it is one of his signature handheld cones or an elaborate parlor model, each one is a perfect example of why kaleidoscopes are not just kaleidoscopes; they are works of art.

Charles began a focused trial and error, self-teaching approach to kaleidoscopes in 1979, and has progressed steadily, with patience and determination, to attain the highest standard of excellence. His award-winning work is appreciated by peers and collectors alike for superior optics, seamless images, and impressive exteriors. He has created more than a dozen different mirror systems, ranging from three to twenty-four inches in length, and producing from two to twenty points in the mandala, each with a unique exterior. Charles works alone in his Maryland studio making every piece himself, from the intricate shards of hand-worked glass in the dry object cells to the smoothly fused glass exteriors, which are as pleasing to the hand as to the eye.

Golf and friends occupy the major portion of Charles' leisure time. He is happiest and most comfortable on a golf course or interacting with his friends. The qualities of balance and variety are reflected in his philosophy as well as his activities and skill. In his own words, "Kaleidoscopes represent what is important in a harmonious life—great diversity living together in one place, creating order out of chaos."

12-point image

Trigon image

0

Trigon

Duo Delta

Kaleidoscopes by Tom and Carol Paretti were considered to be avant-garde in the late 1970s. Their kaleidoscopes continue to be innovative at the beginning of the twenty-first century. And to think it all started with a Cracker Jack™ box! After taking the kaleidoscope prize apart to discover the secret behind the magic, Tom made a kaleidoscope for his design class project. The rest of Working Wood's story is an important part of kaleidoscope history.

The Parettis make every piece of their kaleidoscopes by hand in their northern Arizona studio. For several years they worked exclusively with exotic woods. Then they started using leather, anodized aluminum, and Pyrex™ glass filled with tiny glass beads for the barrels, reserving the finely hewn and highly polished wood for the eyepieces, turning ends, and their hallmark wood fluting for the third side of the mirror system. Whatever material is used, they maintain the quality of their work at the highest standard, and are respected for meticulous craftsmanship.

Tom and Carol have adhered to their own guidelines: to use variations of bright color, change and randomness in the image, a good optical system, a proper relationship of the size of the chamber to the mirror system, lots of imagination, plus important intangibles that even they can't define—but which add up to "Wow!"

"I think our goal is mainly to amuse ourselves with our new ideas," Carol confides. "It is extra fun when we are able to share a new idea with our customers and see from the smiles on their faces that they are as fascinated as we are. It is also exciting to give the viewer free rein to create their own image from the playful items we provide in the object cell."

Slow Yo-Yo scopes and image photos by Melani W

Starfield image. Photo by Adam Peiperl

Sparks image. Photo by Adam Peiperl

Curvaceous (series 640 variation)

Glenn Straub

Glenn Straub has achieved the highest degree of optical excellence, and is recognized as a master of mirror cutting. By borrowing the best from the past and adding au courant expertise, Glenn creates what he hopes will become treasured antique scopes of the future. For many years his son Ben worked as a partner in Wood You Believe, a trade name which came about via tool/die making and precision woodworking, and together they designed traditional style scopes characterized by the simplicity and naturalness of their Pennsylvania Dutch countryside.

Glenn and Ben rank among the few who have perfected the technique of making hermetically sealed liquid-filled ampules, and were the first to introduce a polarized liquid-filled ampule. The resulting imagery from these rare hand-blown objects excite exclamations such as, "Electrifying! Awesome! Sensational! Invigorating!"

Mandalas have long interested Glenn as a way of centering and meditating. "The optical symmetry of the mandala," Glenn asserts, "helps man to emerge from a closely personal experience in order to reach a comprehensive view of the universal. It enables the viewer to expand beyond himself. Creating kaleidoscopes remains my contribution to the unity of the diverse."

Phoenix Parlour image

Image through a polarized-filter scope

Cresere (one-of-a-kind). Photo by Gary Landsman

S. F. Polarized Parlour Scope. Photo by Gary Alcorn

Sherry Moser

Inquisitive and intuitive vie with caring and giving to best describe the real Sherry Moser. When Sherry was a kid she was certain that she had no artistic talent at all, but she always loved color and stained glass, especially dichroic glass. Convinced that her fascination with dichroic glass stemmed from her artist father's occupation as a neon tube bender, Sherry points out the similarity between electric neon colors and the vibrant tones of dichroic glass.

Although she was a pediatric oncology nurse in her first career, it didn't take Sherry long to develop her latent creative ability. She realized that stained glass, combined with the right colors, light, and form, could be transformed into beautiful pieces of art. Soon she was making her own innovative advances in the kaleidoscopes world, with many of her pieces winning awards for their originality, craftsmanship, and universal appeal. Sherry is among the few artists who have mastered the superb technique of making liquid-filled ampules. She is also the first, if not only, artist to inject a dry cell containing liquid-filled ampules into a larger liquid cell.

Appreciative of the generous sharing and helpfulness of fellow scope artists during her early days of scope-making, Sherry now relishes the role of mentor herself, and takes delight in sharing techniques, sources, and ideas. A light within seems to brighten her every encounter. "I think the whole community benefits from sharing," Sherry contends, "if someone's work can be better, it helps the entire community."

What's the Point? image

Dreamdrops image

Kalalani

The Portal

Painted endpiece for **Dreamdrops**

Peggy and Steve Kittelson

Peggy and Steve Kittelson greet life with a smile. In fact, it would be a rare moment indeed to find either one of them without a smile. Their happy expression springs from an inner source of spiritual heritage as well as their enthusiasm for living. Life on an Iowa farm keeps them attuned to the flora and fauna that they lovingly infuse into their kaleidoscopes.

Singing and baking are two of Peggy's favorite non-scope activities, and Steve opts for reading or spending time with family and friends in his off-hours. But most of their time is spent designing and perfecting their award-winning kaleidoscopes. Fused glass is the main medium for both the barrels and cell objects of their collectible pieces. Peggy's tiny torch-worked flowers rank among the most beautiful objects of all to be viewed through a kaleidoscope.

Revealing their metaphysical connection with scopes, Peggy insists that, "Kaleidoscope images are like precious moments in time that we must cherish, because once they are gone, we can never get them back." Steve adds, "They are also like people—they come in a wide variety of exteriors but only by looking inside do you see the true beauty unfolding."

Tapestry Unfolds image

Inside Out image

Inside Out

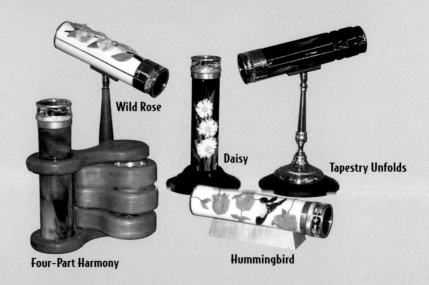

Wild Rose

Four-Part Harmony

Daisy

Tapestry Unfolds

Hummingbird

There is emotional significance in every color, and you feel them all when you look into a kaleidoscope by Randy and Shelley Knapp. They seem to breathe life into their scopes. The combination of Randy's woodworking and Shelley's glass-torch work make for a real dream team. They were among the first to produce a kaleidoscope using a black background with a side-lit object cell. This continues to be one of the most popular of all types, used for both liquid and dry cells, and is now employed by a large percentage of scope artists. The Knapps were also first to introduce a "roof prism" with dichroic windows, allowing light to enter from the front and side. This ensures unsurpassed colors.

Randy's favorite aspect of scope-making is designing new models. In fact, he also likes to work with materials that are new for him. Having achieved a reputation as one of the leading wood scope artists, he switched to blowing glass. Then, becoming proficient in that medium as well, he moved back to exotic woods. And although wood is closest to Randy's heart, it may well be that the capstone of his work is the "Marbleator." That piece, in an edition of three, was the culmination of his brief sojourn with glass marbles.

Marbleator. Photo by Gary Landsman

Shelley is thrilled to have created her very own lamp-worked glass "Lucinis." Each of these tiny, refined, and detailed pieces is a little color sculpture in itself. Floating in a cell, it produces a powerful image. The use of a metallic marbleizing technique renders the exterior of Shelley's scopes as visually stimulating as the interior.

These self-taught artists admit they derive much of their inspiration from the sun-swept splendor of their native Oregon coast. It is their earnest wish that their kaleidoscopes "excite the mind and tingle the imagination of appreciative viewers through generations to come."

Image through a kaleidoscope with **Lucinis** by Shelley

Prismarized image. Photo by Adam Peiperl

Variations

Kalos

One-of-a-kinds. Photo by John Woodin

Integration

Luc and Sallie Durette

Luc and Sallie Durette are an unassuming couple with an unsurpassed line of kaleidoscopes. Eminently successful in blending optical engineering and sculpted art into functional beauty, Luc and Sallie are always looking toward new horizons, new experiences, and new designs. From simple handheld scopes, to sophisticated and complex table models with extra cells, wheels, and barrels that contain different mirror systems, their work is powerful and evocative.

Luc's education in the sciences together with his woodworking and glass skills lend precision and innovation to their award-winning kaleidoscopes. Sallie contributes her painting, calligraphy and graphic arts skills to their work, and son Noah, who put in his appearance in 1995, adds the crown jewel to their joint venture.

Working together in the magical world of kaleidoscopes in their own little bit of Pacific Northwest "utopia wetlands," the Durettes are following a fortune cookie suggestion, "Set your sights high and go for it." With two creeks, ten bridges, hundreds of rhododendrons, and numerous horticultural delights on their property, it is no wonder they have chosen Secret Garden Kaleidoscopes for their company name. Luc and Sallie agree that, "Through our work we hope to provide others with a tool that can be used in the external world to reach that vast and glorious garden within."

Eclipse image. Photo by Tom Ferguson

Cell filled with Durette's lamp-worked pieces. Photo by Tom Ferguson

Bali Hai Botanicals

Firedance, Eclipse, Shadowdance

Christmas series

David Collier

"Creative ideas for exploring minds" is the apt motto for the Oregon-based kaleidoscope business of David and Terry Collier. A love for wood, a degree in industrial business, and an inventive mind all help David accomplish his goal: "To produce premier-quality scopes at a reasonable price, so that everyone can enjoy the beauty of select hardwoods in magnificent handcrafted pieces." David describes his favorite hobby as "life," his idea of beauty as "any person or thing that can be tolerated for more than one hour," and his greatest accomplishment as being "in progress."

Current line of Collier scopes

Rainbow Storm image

Voyager 2000 image

Orbiter image

Voyager 2000
(The object is a 35-mm hand-painted film that
transfers from one reel to another with a turn of
the side knob; the sides are hand-marbled fabric.)

Orbiter

Harmony

Bob and Grace Ade

A close friend describes Bob and Grace Ade as two very interesting and talented soul-mates with a zest for life. Registering high in their zest zone are a passion for travel and a devotion to their children and grandchildren. Certainly their amazing progress in the realm of kaleidoscopes is yet another example of their zest. When they first started making simple glass scopes in the mid-1980s in remote Abingdon, Virginia, they didn't have a clue as to the complex and sophisticated models they would someday be unveiling at Brewster Society conventions.

Bob defines beauty as "nature's wonders, large and small." When they moved to the Puget Sound area of Washington State, a nightly view of the North Star inspired Bob to work on a mirror system that would capture the mystique of that brilliant star. Sure enough, Bob's true colors, and those of the North Star, shine through his highly original "Crystal Star," the third piece in an on-going "Crystal" series.

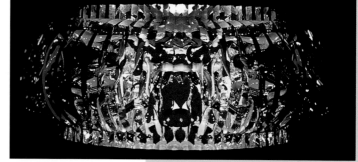

Teuquet image

Glass continues to be the Ades' medium, both in the bodies and the lamp-worked pieces for the object cells. But their focus has switched to complex mirror configurations and variations of the polyangular mirror system, "Polar Ice" being a polarized parlor model. Normally this system consists of two mirrors, one fixed and the other movable, creating a variable number of segments or points. In "Diamonds," however, Bob has introduced a four-mirror system, and all four mirrors move, which forms a changing diamond-shaped central image. Kudos to the Ades for their significant contributions in the kaleidoscope arena.

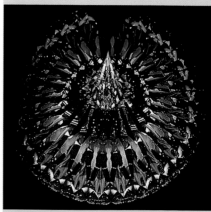

Crystal Pillar image

Diamonds image

Diamonds (double polyangular)

Crystal Point

Crystal Star

Bob McWilliam

Photo by Donna McWilliam

Kaleidoscopes provide a happy career for retired army colonel, helicopter pilot, and hospital administrator Bob McWilliam. Channeling his keen interest in art, woodworking, glass, and design into this one creative art form has been the perfect vent for Bob's adventurous spirit and relaxed attitude. The biggest challenge for his new endeavor was to find a style or design distinctly his own. Everyone who owns a colorful McWilliam one-of-a-kind wood and glass kaleidoscope will attest to its distinctiveness.

While grandchildren vie with scopes for Bob's attention these days, both manage to get their fair share. Bob spends eight hours a day in his San Antonio studio where he makes every part of his scope, matching stand, and glass object pieces (including liquid-filled ampules) by hand. Each of Bob's object cells opens to permit a change or inclusion of personal objects. A special feature in some models is a set of filters that allows a change of the background colors. "Kaleidoscopes have opened new vistas and been wonderful for me," Bob says. "They've given me an outlet to exercise my artistic talents, and while I feel I've made some minor contributions to the art, I have to admit that the kaleidoscope world has given far more to me than I've given to it."

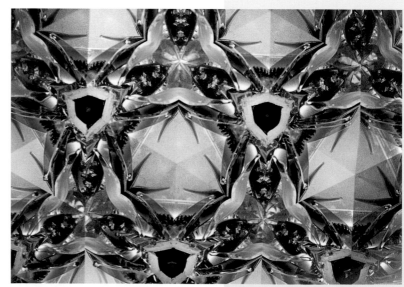

Image through three-mirror system

Image through three-mirror system

Parlor scope with two barrels

Wood and stained-glass parlor scope

Ken and Dore Wilhoite

Ken and Dore Wilhoite love to be together. In 1999 they left the corporate world—where they worked at the same aerospace company for more than ten years—to become fulltime kaleidoscope artists. They made their first scope in 1990 as a home metal shop project, and were so pleased with the result that they set out to learn all they could about the design and construction of kaleidoscopes. On the way they learned that they also loved to be with many of the people who make, sell, and collect kaleidoscopes.

Dore went about "adopting" several scope artists to be her brothers and sisters. In fact her kaleido-family now almost outnumbers her penguin family (an earlier obsession resulting in a record-breaking collection). Whatever Dore takes on she tackles with enthusiasm, and she's never happier than when she is doing something to make someone else happy.

A combination of polished brass and aluminum distinguishes the entire line of Wilhoite kaleidoscopes. Sleek hand-held tubes and sculptured geometric shapes, all with matching stands, gleam with contrasting gold and silver tones. Ken takes great pride in fine tuning and refining his work, always looking for ways to improve both the machining and lamp-working. He is also always ready to offer suggestions or a helping hand to new artists as an appreciative way of compensating for the advice and help he has received from so many others.

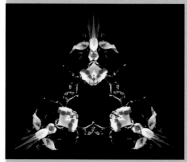

Little Luni image. Photo by Adam Peiperl

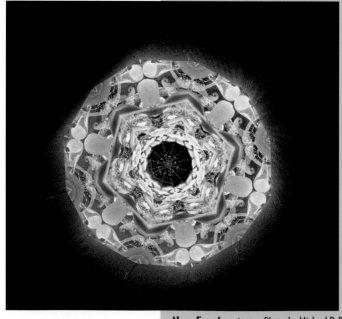

New Freedom image. Photo by Michael P. Richardso

American Freedom image. Photo by Adam Peiperl

Little Luni
Photo by Adam Peiperl

American Freedom
Photo by Adam Peiperl

New Freedom
Photo by Michael P. Richardson

Image through dichroic wheels by Janice and Ray Chesnik

CHAPTER

Wheels, Cylinders, and Carousels

Collage by Sue Ross

Kaleidoscopes exhibit a remarkable sense of being alive,
just a heart pulse beyond each changing image.

Millefiori wheel by Janice and Ray Chesnik

$\mathcal{W}$heels were the first objective endpieces introduced as an alternate to the object chamber, or cell. Kaleidoscopes with wheels for the object to be viewed were the big trend in the 1980s.

In my first book about kaleidoscopes, *Through the Kaleidoscope* (1985), it was pointed out that there are more varieties of the two-wheel kaleidoscope than of any other type: giant wheels, miniature wheels, glass wheels, agate wheels, a combination of agate and glass, acrylic wheels, wheels embedded with dried flowers, gem-encrusted wheels, wheels made of "found objects," and even gear-powered wheels.

At first only one wheel was used for the object. Then a second, third, even a fourth and fifth wheel were added.

To create an interesting image, the number of different-shaped pieces and distinctive types of glass that are used in each wheel is more important than the number of wheels used. Cylinders (sometimes referred to as spinners) and carousels are stylish variations of the traditional fixed or hollow wheels.

Star Explosion by Corki Weeks

Janice and Ray Chesnik

The Chesniks were among the first to popularize the wheel scope. As partners in the early 1980s, Janice and her daughter Sheryl Koch helped make kaleidoscope history. Later they each formed their own company, and Janice joined forces with husband Ray and son Jon. Good is not good enough, and neither is approval from others for these professionals who continue to learn from what they do and keep making improvements. With a determination and discipline unmatched, Chesnik Scopes has earned a reputation as one of the most dedicated and best-organized of any kaleidoscope company. Indeed, they are respected by peers and retailers alike for their stellar example of business combined with art.

Fascinated with color since her first crayons and intrigued with all things made of glass, Janice sees to it that every wheel on their wide variety of scope bodies is exceptional in both color and texture. This means using high-tech dichroic glass, and mastering the centuries-old Italian glass art process of *millefiori* pattern bar slices. They have accomplished this with special kilns and large furnaces at their Southern California home-based studio.

Millefiori wheel

When they aren't keeping their nose to that proverbial grindstone, you might find Janice in the garden, Ray cooking up something great, or the whole fun-loving family off traveling to some interesting spot.

The role of mentor is one that Janice enjoys as well, and the number of fellow scope artists that she and Ray have encouraged to find their special niche would be hard to determine. But many are the voices that sing their praise. Appreciative of the beauty of kaleidoscopes as well as the creativity in making them, Janice is always inspired when she watches someone looking through one of their scopes. "The smiles and delight that come over their faces is the tonic that keeps me going," she says. "Like kaleidoscopes themselves, people are a joy!"

Fiesta image

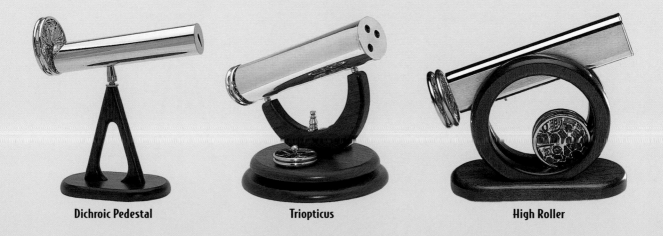

Dichroic Pedestal

Triopticus

High Roller

Sheryl Koch

Sheryl Koch is quiet and unassuming, but the images in her kaleidoscopes are bold and dynamic. Admittedly a visual person, Sheryl enjoys spectacular vistas where she lives in Washington State as well as inside her scopes. She is credited with originating the double-image "Gemini" four-mirror system, and also the surprising "Eclipse" image. But probably the greatest surprise for entrepreneur Koch has been the big business kaleidoscopes have become, and the important role the extended kaleidoscope family has played in her life. "It's been a wonderful environment in which to raise my daughter," she says, smiling, "we both feel blessed."

Eclipse image

Trinity image

Trinity

Mary Theresa Boll

Mary Boll is an artist who is interested in power; not the kind that seeks to dominate another, but the power that is generated through our thoughts, wishes, hopes, and dreams. For twenty-six years Mary has taught art to kids of all ages, from three to eighty-three. She teaches because she feels a need to share knowledge and to challenge others with knowledge. She makes kaleidoscopes because that is what she likes to do.

As a kaleidoscope collector, Mary was not able to find a kaleidoscope that incorporated fiber-art textures, so in 1990 she set about, with determination, to design her own woven-wheel scopes. She also started making kaleidoscopes for Christmas tree ornaments after being asked to contribute one for the White House Christmas tree.

The mention of a "circular arrangement of the images of a candle round a centre" in Brewster's *Treatise on the Kaleidoscope*, inspired yet another design, "Brewster's Fire." Constructed of stained glass, this tribute to the inventor, made in two sizes, contains a carousel to hold candles. In the large size, there are two carousels, the inner one attached to a music box which turns automatically, and the outer one moved manually so the viewer can control the image.

Brewster's Fire

Mary enjoys watching others look through kaleidoscopes almost as much as she loves to look through them herself. "Kaleidoscopes feed my soul," she says. "I find that looking into one is like looking through a small window into a vast world. It is also something I can share with others." And she always adds as a pivotal part of her signature, "Leave no scope unturned!"

Fiber wheel scopes

"Infinite Visions," the name of one of hundreds of scopes by Corki Weeks, aptly characterizes this multitalented artist. Throughout numerous artistic endeavors, Corki has utilized her keen eye for design. Prior to kaleidoscopes, her vision centered on weaving, pottery, jewelry, baskets, clothing, and stained glass. Since turning all her attention to scopes in 1983, Corki has produced close to 150,000 kaleidoscopes. The impact of this number, in terms of generating scope awareness and enthusiasm, is hard to measure.

Corki's generosity of spirit and influence on fellow artists is also tremendous. She is one of the most admired of all the scope artists. To quote one fellow artist, "Corki makes scopes that every scope-maker wishes he had made—sleek, beautiful and affordable, with easily interchangeable cells." Another scope by Corki, "The Last Hurrah," contains her original concept that prompted the first Brewster Society Award for Creative Ingenuity— two different mirror systems in the same tube.

While working on as many as twenty different models at one time in her Colorado studio, Corki continues to hone and refine every aspect of kaleidoscope production. This includes experimenting with various and complex mirror arrangements. "But," Corki confides, "in my twenty years of scope-making and struggling to find new or different mirror systems I have decided nothing beats a regular two-mirror image. It is fun to look into an unusual mirror set-up, but for moments of true enjoyment, nothing is better than the traditional two-mirror mandala."

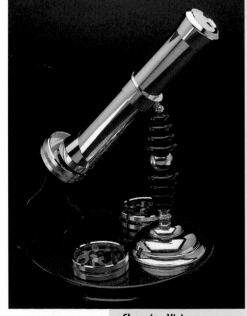

Changing Visions

Star Explosion II image

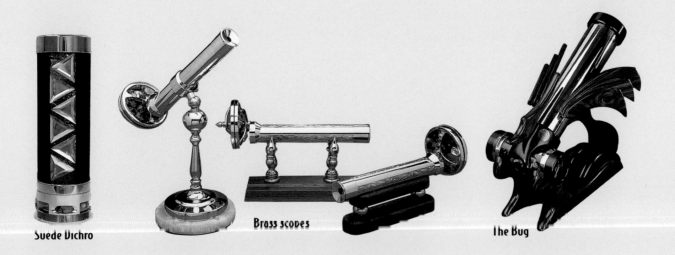

Suede Dichro

Brass scopes

The Bug

Sue Ross feels sure that kaleidoscopes will someday be found on Mars! If she is right, it is certain that more than one scope will reveal the signature of Sue Ross. The variety and diversity of her kaleidoscopes manifest the very words that Sue chose when asked to define herself in just five words: free spirit, complex, curious, creative, and goal-oriented! It's hard for Sue to decide which brings her more inner peace and happiness: experimenting with her glass and kiln or working in her flower garden.

Sue first started making marble scopes, soon changed to wheels, then carousels and spinners. She also introduced embroidery with silk ribbon, and her latest venture is designing garden metal sculpture and arc welding. A quote from the famous artist Georgia O'Keeffe could have been a personal quote from Sue: "I found I could say things with color and shapes that I couldn't say in any other way. Things I had no words for." But the future is something that Sue does have words for, "Even after seventeen years, I've really just begun. I want to continue chasing the winds of my dreams to a free-spirited perch on a rainbow!"

Carousel scopes

Artistic grouping of various Ross scopes

Susan's Garden floral ribbon embroidery scopes

Dragonfly

Robert Cook and Jocelyn Teh

Each kaleidoscope that Robert Cook and Jocelyn Teh create is a beautiful and complex sculpture in and of itself. They design and produce these works of art in their native Australia, under the name Arcana Kaleidoscopes. While great skill is applied to each and every detail of the intricate construction, it is for the ancient art process of patination that Robert is widely recognized and appreciated. The term *patineur* is of French origin and describes an artist whose craft is the aesthetic coloring and manipulation of metals through secret oxidation processes. The tradition of coloring copper and its many alloys is used by few, if any, other scope artists.

After years of experimenting with the application, heat, oils, and acids, Robert has learned to use a wide range of extraordinary patinas that excite the eye, evoke emotion, and inspire interpretation. Two rotating wheels are used as the object to be viewed in their copper, brass, and bronze scopes, and more than sixteen different mirror systems have been employed. They take great pride in the quality of agates and gemstones selected for their wheels, finding and digging many themselves. The clutch (or gear-driven turning mechanism) is yet another unique (and patented) element to be found in each Arcana kaleidoscope.

A dual fascination with Victorian scientific instruments and antique books, evident in every nook and corner of Robert and Jocelyn's treasure-trove home, adds another note of validity to this vivacious couple's total involvement in the kaleidoscope world. Their interests, passions, and professional pursuits run the gamut, and are as varied and satisfying as the images in their intriguing instruments.

Two Swans

Image through one-of-a-kind scope. Photo by Adam Peiperl

On Eagle's Wings

Universal Horseless Traction Engine

The Carousel

Drummer Boy

Donald E. Ballwey

As an associate professor of glass at California State University, Don Ballwey teaches all facets of stained glass, including how to make kaleidoscopes. Unique to Don's scopes are his cast and stamped-glass jewels, which he has been making for more than a decade. Don carves permanent molds of carbon by hand, then pours molten glass into them, pressing the glass into the mold with a paddle. He then cuts each jewel with a glass cutter, and solders the jewels into either the body of the scope or one of the wheels.

The Tutankhamen Exhibition inspired Don Ballwey to craft some scopes with a strong Egyptian influence. He uses black iridescent glass to represent the black fertile soil surrounding the Nile, and vibrant blues and purples associated with ancient Egyptian royalty. "One of my goals," Don admits, "is to have not only the present collectors enjoy my work, but also to have their great-great-great-great-grandchildren get the same enjoyment."

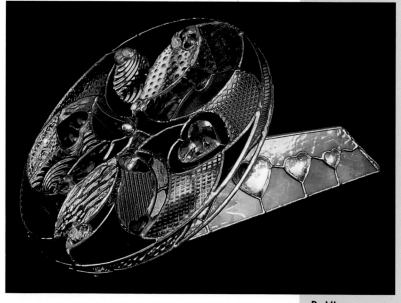

Be Mine

Wheel

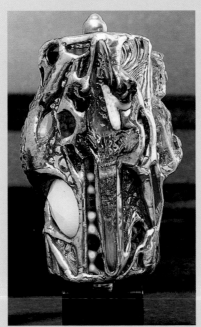

Spinner

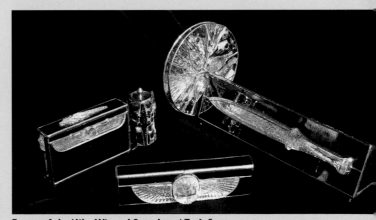

Facets of the Nile, Winged Scarab, and Tut's Scope

Bob and Sue Rioux

Photo by Brad Maushart

Enthusiasm and fun are contagious around Bob and Sue Rioux. Whether it involves fresh lobster from the waters of their native Maine, or a scope they are designing as a special gift for former president and neighbor George Bush, these ambitious artists exude energy and exuberance. Even their creative thirteen-year-old son Alex designs and makes kaleidoscopes, winning the People's Choice "Rookie" award at the 1998 Brewster Society convention.

Award winners themselves, Bob and Sue are adventurous in their lifestyle as well as their art. They have made dramatic changes in their jobs (from banking and construction to kaleidoscopes), location (from Maine to California and back to Maine), and an unlikely alternate to their basic medium of glass is Paperclay®. This choice isn't as strange as it seems, however, nor are the resultant humorous life-size figures of "Aunt Sylvia" and "Clifford," when you realize that Sue was sculpting whimsical figures as far back as the fourth grade.

The goal of Sea Parrot (the Rioux's company, named after their Maine locale and talkative pets) is to keep moving forward creatively while maintaining superior quality in all of their work. They are also dedicated to helping and encouraging fellow scope artists, and to promoting the positive aspects of kaleidoscopes to the world.

Maude

Aunt Sylvia

Gold Rush image by Adam Peiperl

Egret. Photos of scopes by Chris Smith

Whale Dance

Summer Evening and **Spring Morning**

David Piper

David Piper, a Pennsylvania native who now lives in Oaxaca, Mexico, had a varied career before he started making kaleidoscopes full time. He was a machinist, boat builder, crop-duster pilot, Honolulu taxi driver, marine biologist, and shrimp farmer. He always loved kaleidoscopes, even the cardboard and plastic toy variety. When he chanced to find some rather ornate scopes in a New Orleans gallery a few years ago, he felt inspired to try his hand at making some. Just one problem: He had no idea how to begin. After learning about the Brewster Society, David drove three thousand miles from the south of Mexico to Corning, New York, to attend the 1996 annual convention. "Properly humbled by the artistry and craftsmanship I saw," David recalls, "I went back to Oaxaca to apply the skills I have in wood- and metal-working toward creating my own [scopes]."

David's designs are derived from the textiles and woodcarvings of the Zapotec and Mixtec Indian cultures that have flourished in his area for centuries, and are made from local salvaged hardwoods, silver, dried flowers, butterfly wings, amber, and semiprecious stones. "My goal is to make the best kaleidoscope that my abilities allow," he says. "When my eight-year-old daughter tells me, 'Daddy, that's beautiful,' I can hope I'm getting close."

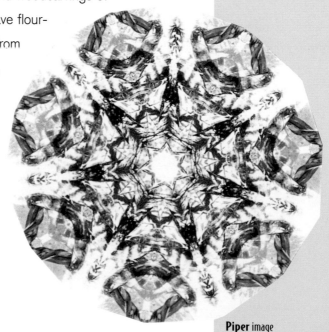

Piper image

Inlaid box with scope and extra wheels

Inlaid wood chest with scope and wheels

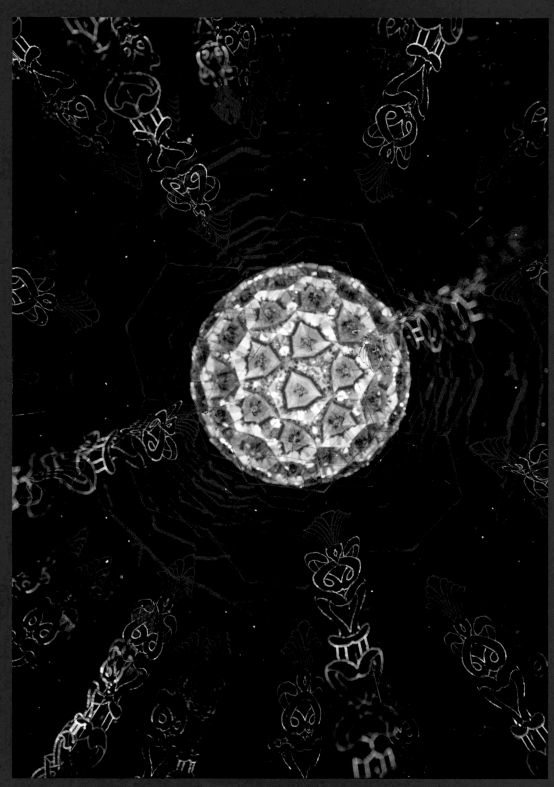

Experiment image by David Sugich

Marbles and Tubes

Gigantic Planet by Debbie and David Rosenfeldt

Looking at the world through rose-colored glasses gives but
a faint glow compared to looking through a kaleidoscope—
it kindles dreams and ignites imagination.

Orbitron, base of waterfalls scope by Will Smith

$\mathcal{M}$ arbles are a natural object for the endpiece of a kaleidoscope. They turn easily and look pretty even before being viewed through a mirror system. But as with all objects, the more complex and colorful the marble, the greater the image. A simple pattern, even a latticino swirl, tends to be repetitious. On the other hand, although interesting and intricate, a Josh Simpson "Planet" proves too dense for good scope viewing. To assure a pleasing and satisfying image a few artists make their own marbles, and include different textures along with air bubbles to enhance the image.

Probably no other object placed at the end of a kaleidoscope has realized such a sudden and widespread acceptance as the space tube. WildeWood Creative Products, in collaboration with Cozy Baker, produced the initial concept with their "Illusion," followed soon by almost everyone who ever produced any kind of scope. And there were rip-offs from here to Taiwan and back. But there were also a few artists who added a significant element to make their own special mark with this popular type of scope.

Blue Parlor Scope by Debbie and David Rosenfeldt

David Sugich

"Exuberant" is the best word to describe David Sugich and his kaleidoscopes. He has synthesized his background of music and crafts into the visual music that virtually defines the kaleidoscope. Inspired by WildeWood's "Illusion" (the first scope to use liquid-filled tubes as the object to be viewed), David has elevated the "tube" scope to new heights. Building on the wonderful dynamics of the directional flow of simultaneous explosions and implosions, he has developed a whole series. One style uses the tube as the base or third side of the mirrored triangle. In others he utilizes the background on which to etch vibrant flowers, sparkling fireflies or radiant angels.

Ultimate Reflections is the appropriate name of David and his wife Nadareh's kaleidoscope business. They both view the continued birth and death of infinite images within the kaleidoscope to be a reminding and healing metaphor. The words of "Kaleidoscope," a song composed by David Sugich, really sums up their kaleidoscope philosophy:

Amazing reflections
Crystal perfections
In dazzling directions of colorful flow!
Enchanting, surprising
Setting and rising
Uncompromising in a circular show!

Chorus:
The sun, moon, stars, and the rain
Weaving their seasons again and again
Ensuing, renewing, a prayer and a hope
Inside a kaleidoscope

As the image dances
The picture enhances
and easily balances expressively
Mandala unbroken,
Magical token
How long have you spoken so effortlessly?

An angel's confession
In stunning succession
Unfolding her blessing
Revealing her way
Forever renewing a prayer and a hope
Inside this kaleidoscope

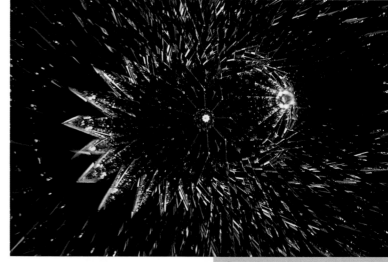

Peacock image

Temple image (convex)

Temple image (concave)

Temple

Debbie and David Rosenfeldt

"We give kaleidoscopes shape and color and they in turn give us balance and beauty." That is the philosophy of Debbie and David Rosenfeldt, who also believe that kaleidoscopes can help one discover the inherent harmony in all beings. Like many of the artists, Deb and David were collecting scopes long before they started making them. Unlike others, however, David decided on an entirely new medium for his scopes. Tired of sawdust, he tried several materials, including anodized aluminum, before settling on glass.

They named their business "Shipwrecked" because for many years it was their dream to be shipwrecked on a tropical island. With the arrival in 1998 of a beaming baby boy (appropriately named Sterling Blue), their dream may have changed somewhat, but not the ardor and zeal with which they conduct business. A recent decision to change the type and style of scopes they had been making for about seven years was a good one. Wheels gave way to liquid orbs, and stained glass was replaced with blown glass.

They put their heart and soul into each piece, and a special energy seems to glow right through their lustrous dichroic kaleidoscopes. "David is never happier than when blowing glass," Deb confides, "and the best part about making kaleidoscopes for me is the people we've met and the friends we've made. Also, what a joy on Christmas morning to know that people are opening up kaleidoscopes all over the world."

Close-up of five-inch liquid marble

Parlette, Moe, and **Purple Parlor**

Kelley

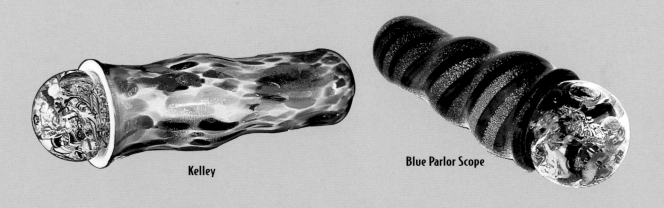

Blue Parlor Scope

Six different sized marbles

Henry Bergeson

Photo by Michael E. Fulks

A gentle glow of grandeur shines through each kaleidoscope designed and engineered by Henry Bergeson. The care and love he puts into each scope can be felt as well as seen in the smoothly sensuous well-polished hardwoods he selects for his innovative pieces of art.

Studying and working on old boats in New England dominated Henry's early years. Then in 1979, he set sail with his father from Norway to Maine in a forty-two foot 1905 yawl. The voyage ended in disaster when their vessel was mortally damaged six hundred miles south of Iceland. He and his father were rescued, but the boat was left to drift off into the fog. This catastrophic experience changed Henry's outlook on life. From then on, conformity and the rigors of corporate life loomed inconsequential, and a more relaxed and individual hands-on type work became his focus.

The environment provided by the Colorado mountains has proved a happy choice for Henry's home and studio. He feels that all of his previous experiences and circumstances have somehow inexorably woven themselves into the kaleidoscopes he makes. "I like my own environment for sure," Henry says, "I like to make things, and I like to make nice things." And that he does!

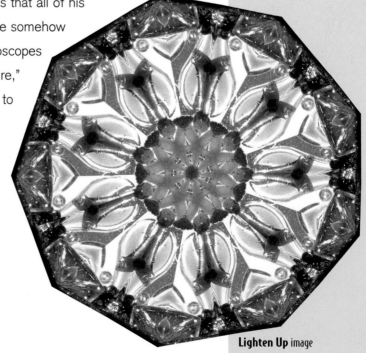

Lighten Up image

Why Not 2K? image. Photos by Michael E. Fulks

Lighten Up

The Marble Scope

Why Not 2K?

The light that shines brightly inside B. T. Ansley IV glows right through his kaleidoscopes. Ben makes all of his kaleidoscopes from alabaster. When the library at Yale University was built, the engineers wanted the most perfect light possible. They decided on translucent alabaster windows, because the light passing through them was as close as they could come to perfection. What better material, then, through which to view kaleidoscopes? The subtle diffusion of the light by the alabaster creates an ethereal environment for the Venetian *millefiori* and dichroic glass that Ben uses for the colorful objects to be viewed.

For twenty-five years before he started making scopes, Ben pursued a business career while at the same time serving as artist-in-residence at Cameron University in Lawton, Oklahoma. He was also a regular army officer and paratrooper, and is now a private pilot, gourmet cook, and collector of fine wines.

"It was the beauty of the people making kaleidoscopes," Ben admits, "as much as the beauty of the scopes themselves that really inspired me to get back into the art world." And it was a recent personal experience that prompted Ben to create a kaleidoscope as a statement of his faith. He explains, "The theme song 'De Colores' (the Colors of Christ) at an Emmaus retreat (a nondenominational group for study and prayer) along with my newly found faith inspired the 'Cross Kaleidoscope.' The fact that light is able to penetrate so brightly such dense stone remains a beautiful mystery to me, and is a profound part of the creative imagery in this kaleidoscope."

Medium Double Head

Alabaster scopes

Phil Coghill

Phil Coghill has been producing kaleido-scopes in his Louisiana studio since 1988. A background in industrial arts gave Phil the technical skills needed to design and construct kaleidoscopes. A yearning for artistic expression, together with his love for glass and wood, provide the impetus to create kaleidoscopes that are decorative as well as entertaining. Their ability to stimulate the mind is equally rewarding to Phil, who also enjoys the challenge of experimenting with different mirror systems and various ways to turn the object case. Future plans include sculptural shapes that don't resemble tradi-tional kaleidoscopes. "In these scopes," Phil explains, "the exterior is the first consideration and the interior image is just a *lagniappe* (a cajun term for a little something extra)."

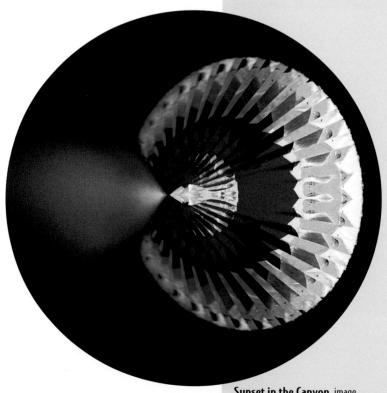

Sunset in the Canyon image

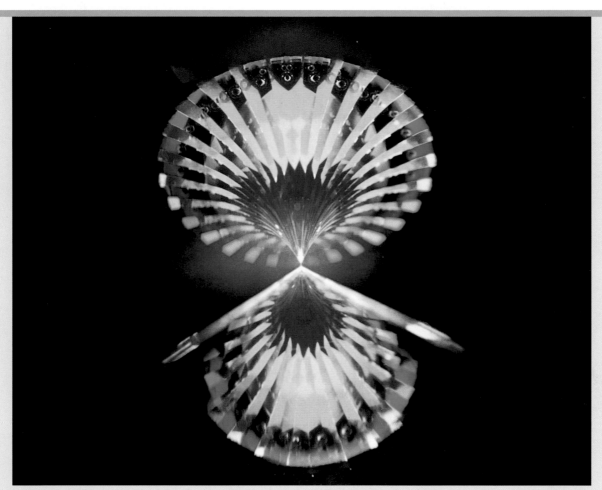

Moon Over the Bayou image

Y and **K** scopes with flat tube

Sunset in the Canyon and **Moon over the Bayou**

Flat tube object case

Passport to Paris image by Judith Paul and Tom Durden

Objects and Theme Scopes

Lighthouse by David Kalish. Photo by Douglas Campbell

Kaleidoscopes open onto expanded horizons
where fantasy and reality merge and interact.

Although the body of the kaleidoscope is usually structured in classic geometric shapes, there is a growing number of artists who utilize the contour of popular objects, such as an egg, airplane, train, lighthouse, hot-air balloon, or animal—virtually anything—to create sculptural scopes. Then there are a few who specialize in theme scopes, following through with appropriate object pieces that coordinate with an exciting exterior theme. Still others utilize found objects of all kinds to construct their scopes.

Liberty Egg by Frank Casciani

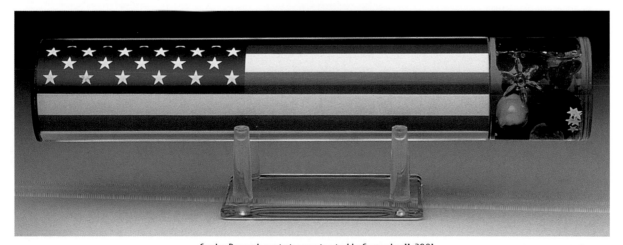

Carolyn Bennett's patriotic scope inspired by September 11, 2001.

David Kalish

Photo by Douglas Campbell

David Kalish has been active in both the visual and performing arts all his life. Since starting his company Chromascope in 1982, David has produced thousands of scopes of many descriptions. Realizing that a kaleidoscope will spend most of its "life" in repose, David approaches his designs as sculptures. He believes the observer should not necessarily recognize that the piece functions as a kaleidoscope. "When that element is discovered," he says with a smile, "the 'oohs' and 'aahs' are as rewarding as a standing ovation. But I think the work should be as captivating and alluring from the outside as from within."

"The Wedding Kaleidoscope" is considered David's signature piece. The original limited edition, made of wood and acrylic, was introduced in 1988. Its unique concept combines two different mirror systems that can be viewed by two people simultaneously from either end. A brass production model of "The Wedding Kaleidoscope" continues to enjoy tremendous popularity, and the term is now used generically to describe any similar configuration of a double-ended kaleidoscope.

Along with a fertile imagination that is prolific in both design and product concepts, David holds definite philosophic ideas relating to the kaleidoscope: "Over time I've come to realize that pattern is the primary stimulus we are responding to. Pattern implies repetition and repetition is essential to all learning. Our minds seek pattern as water seeks its own level. I've seen kaleidophiles forage through kaleidoscopes seeking the 'perfect' image, much like surfers seek to ride the 'perfect' wave . . . .

The Wedding Kaleidoscope

Many people find that the observation of kaleidoscope images is a form of meditation that helps reduce stress and diminish anxiety [see Chapter 8]. Others find it a safe, drug-free way to experience a feeling of euphoria. At the very least, kaleidoscopes are a refreshingly non-electronic source of visual entertainment at our fingertips. And more, they have the capacity to lift and fill our spirits."

Lighthouse and images. All image and scope photos by Douglas Campbell

Odyssey

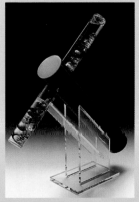

Melting Moments

Brass version of **The Wedding Scope** with **Musette** scope and pendant

Marti Freund

A bird sings because it has a song; Marti Freund makes kaleidoscopes because she has the right gourd. Of course that's not quite all there is to it. Marti started making stained glass and antique mirror teleidoscopes in 1981. Unique decorative "scratchings" and solder filigree designs of animals make them easily recognizable. Not as discernable, but equally important to Marti's handcrafted scopes, are the hand-machined parts made by her father Ed. These include the tiny solid brass washers used between the wheels and others designed to keep tension on the wheels.

To further a heartfelt interest in wildlife, Marti began transforming homegrown gourds into animal kaleidoscopes. Once the scope is soldered into the gourd (or gourds) and the shape of the animal is perfected, Marti paints the figure with acrylic paints, and adds several coats of varnish. She explains, "If looking at an animal 'filigree' or one of my gourds could influence someone to enjoy or respect our wildlife more, that would be the greatest accomplishment I could ever want."

Babaloon

Visions of Down Under gourd scope by Marti Freund

Gourd scope image. Photo by Adam Peiperl

The Emperor's Son

Lookout Hollow

Gourds used to create **Lookout Hollow** and **The Emperor's Son**

Jim and June Mindrup

Husband and wife team Jim and June Mindrup took early retirement and have spent the past ten years making kaleidoscopes. They began making them just to give away. Hundreds were given to children's hospitals and Ronald McDonald Houses for children undergoing treatment for cancer. Their philosophy is very simple: "If our kaleidoscopes can bring a few smiles and magical moments to the children, life has been worthwhile." It was only after the serious urging of collectors to sell their scopes that the Mindrups turned their philanthropic hobby into a commercial venture.

As a team, Jim turns the wood scope parts on a lathe and assembles them, while June, an art major, paints the scopes into colorful, whimsical characters. Great pride in their work is part and parcel of every scope they make. Travels in Russia, where they discovered the enchanting Matrioshka (nesting) dolls and Fabergé eggs, spawned their most popular line of scopes, "Little People" and "Egg-Scope" characters. Lathe-turned, hand-drawn, and hand-painted, each little guy is truly one-of-a-kind.

The Mindrups share a kindred respect for nature's beautiful example of perfection and order in the snow crystal, commonly known as snowflakes. Each one is different, yet all are united by a six-point pattern. They relate this to the kaleidoscope and use a mirror system that best replicates the snowflake's six-point pattern. "When we look deeply into the colorful patterns formed in a kaleidoscope," Jim explains, "we discover rare perfection, incredible order, and miracles of beauty. It brings back the same sense of awe that we once knew as children."

Modest Maiden

Hand-painted characters

Egg scopes

Debra Davis

"If everyone in the world could help one person to smile, we would have a happier, more peaceful planet." Self-taught stained glass artisan Debra Davis practices her own personal reflection, only she has multiplied it hundreds of times. Each of her Stained Glass Originals brings a smile to any person who sees one. The Transportation collection (school bus, train, postal truck, police car, etc.) began as a tribute to her mother, a school-bus driver, and an aunt who drove a postal truck for years. The "Flower Bouquet" collection was born out of her dreams, and the "Sea Vessel" collection—which includes an aircraft carrier, a submarine, and four hospital ships—was inspired by her nine years on active duty in the Navy.

Debra believes that the kaleidoscope's intrigue comes from the anticipation and surprise of each new "wow" as one looks into a scope and turns the object case. Eager to hasten and increase the anticipated surprise, Debra designs scopes that people are amazed to learn are even scopes at all. "Kaleido-Crayons," "Executive Briefcase," "Tee-Time," "Golf Clubs," "Picture This . . .1999" and "Artist's Palette" each tells its own surprising story.

Kaleido-Crayons

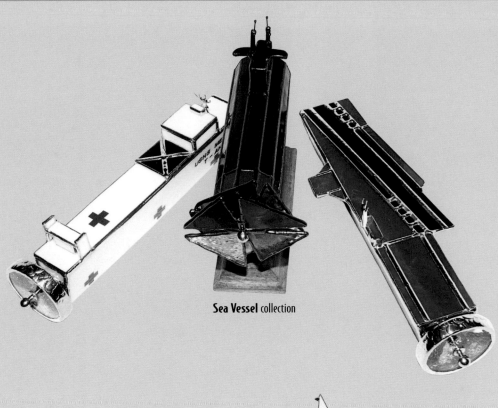

Sea Vessel collection

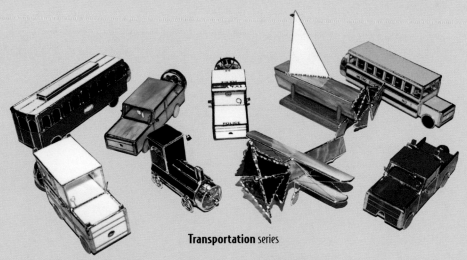

Transportation series

Kaleido-Camera

Joanne and Mike Jacobs

Color looms first and foremost with Joanne Jacobs. Both in her basic love of music (which started with piano lessons at the age of four, culminating in an exciting performance and recording career) and in her more recent passion, stained glass (which developed into working with kaleidoscopes). That was in 1987. Joanne soon became a well-known fixture at the Lincoln Center Crafts festival where she showed her intriguing line of theme scopes, including Jewish scopes as well as dozens of other topics.

Husband Mike, a computer programmer by day, enjoys being an active partner in their Long Island Fantasy Glass business. Their work has been displayed in more than four hundred galleries around the world. Letting the Jacobs' imagination loose on scopes can be likened to letting a kid loose in Santa's workshop. Together they brainstorm ideas and build scopes that are serious fun. Separately, Mike cuts the mirrors, and Joanne creates the cases and object chambers.

"Checkmate," one of their most dramatic creations, is a limited edition kaleidoscope/chess set. Each piece, from pawn to king, is a unique object cylinder that fits into one of two opposing kaleidoscopes. Their own favorite is "Chicken Soup," the scope that's good for you. Combining the artist's love of music and color with homeopathic remedies recommended by her sister, a chiropractor and doctor of homeopathy, it comes with a compact disc of Joanne's original music. It is a treat for the eyes, ears, and more. It is their combined hope that "this scope can help in the healing process, and reflect back the goodwill of the kaleidoscope world."

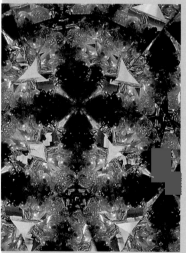

Stardust 2 image

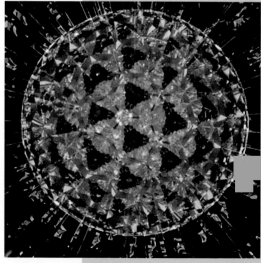

Wind 4 image

Checkmate

Stealth

Riverboat

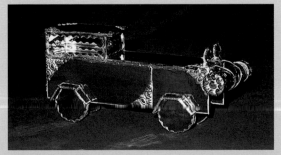

King of the Road

In the Key of Life

Judith Paul and Tom Durden

Judith Paul personifies individuality in her work as well as her lifestyle. Before "kaleidoscope addiction" consumed Judith, she was an art conservator specializing in the restoration of antique paintings and icons. It was her complete absorption with scopes that led to her first design, a collaboration with award-winning scope artist Sherry Moser. Their "Monet Garden" (a limited edition of one hundred) won both the Brewster Society Award for Creative Ingenuity and a People's Choice Award.

Old Gazebo

After this immediate success it didn't take long for Judith to convince husband Tom Durden, recently retired from United Airlines, to be an active partner in making kaleidoscopes. Long a craft enthusiast, with considerable experience in ceramics and fused glass, Tom patiently studied mirror cutting from many of the masters in the field. With perseverance, determination, and a tireless pursuit of excellence, Tom soon developed an expertise that ranks his optics along with the best.

Dolphin

A keen eye for detail and a passion for perfection, along with her background as a studio photographer, ceramist, fabric designer, and glass artist, puts Judith in charge of the company's ideas and designs. As soon as Judith plans one theme she is busy with a new one. And each one sizzles with personality. "Kaleidoscopes seem to me to be one of the few participatory art forms." Judith explains, "I design and supply beautiful objects, balancing line, form, color, and texture, then ask the viewers to turn and tumble them into ever-changing images that please and surprise. Together we all create the beauty." Designing and making their own kaleidoscopes (under the trade name of Images) does not diminish Judith's enthusiasm for collecting the work of others. In her own words, "Collecting as well as designing are both a joy and a discipline."

Fruit of the Vine

Floral image through a three-mirror system

Passport to Paris

It's a Wrap series (fabric florals with cells)

Van Gogh

Frank Casciani

Eggs have been portrayed as the symbol of birth, life, and rebirth for thousands of years. They have also been immortalized as jewelry by goldsmith Peter Carl Fabergé. It is only recently, however, that they have been made into kaleidoscopes. Frank Casciani began egguery in 1990, after retiring from the military. Egguery is, quite simply, using real eggs to create objects of art. No birds are harmed to pursue this art form, and only infertile eggs are used.

Since Frank has always been fascinated with kaleidoscopes, converting eggs into scopes was a natural progression, which he began doing in 1997. The response to his "Designs in Shell" has been tremendous.

Frank acknowledges there is something about the images in a scope that make him feel good. "If I am not feeling happy, I can always lift my spirits by watching the never-ending patterns in one of my kaleidoscopes."

Silver Opal Eggs'Hiliration (Rhea egg)

Egg'Chantment Tea Pot

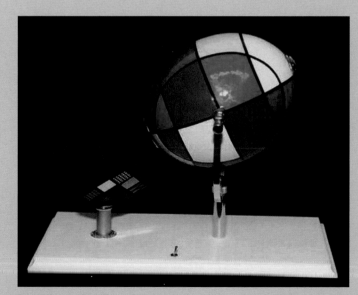

Eggs'Uberant Rub'Eggs (Ostrich egg parlor scope)

Egg'Cessory necklace scopes (Pheasant and Chuker eggs)

Image through necklace kaleidoscope by Massimo Strino

Jewelry and Miniature Scopes

One-of-a-kind miniature scope. Photo by Gary Landsman

Its colors are shards from rainbows
spinning round and round in joyful disguise
Its patterns are the smiles of angels
glowing with beauty in endless surprise

"It's the little things that count" and "expensive things come in small packages" are two clichés that apply to wearable kaleidoscopes. Each standard size scope can be produced in a miniature version, but very few of them are. Probably one of the reasons there are so few is that the smaller they are, the harder they are to make, yet because they take less material and space, they are expected to cost less.

An extraordinary array of miniature scopes can be seen in the stained glass replica of three rooms in Cozy Baker's house/museum, designed and built by stained glass artist Carl Goeller. It was commissioned by Dick and Jackie Pope, chairpersons of the 1996 Brewster Society convention in Corning, New York, and presented to Cozy as a tribute from the membership. Many of the artists made actual working miniature models of their original pieces.

Miniature scopes from the Cozy Baker collection. Photo by Gary Landsman

Massimo Strino

A radiance emanating from within the artist seems to embrace each kaleidoscope created by Massimo Strino. From his childhood in Italy through his bohemian days in Paris where he played a guitar in the subway, Massimo was happiest when making other people happy. In fact, it is the smiles on the faces of those who admire his kaleidoscopes that still provide Massimo his greatest satisfaction.

Massimo takes kaleidoscopes very seriously, and is convinced that through art, humankind will learn how to live in harmony to create a better world for all. He makes scopes of all sizes and shapes, including scepters, with a variety of materials that include Banksia seed-pods. But he is probably best known for his kaleidoscope jewelry. Integrity, originality, simplicity, and understated elegance are the guidelines for each piece, and his objective is for the exterior to surprise and mystify and for the interior to inspire a sense of harmony and tranquility.

Bracelet

Jewel under the Lotus

Image through necklace scope

Gold necklace

Banksia seed-pod scopes

Kevin and Deborah Healy

Kevin and Deborah Healy have been designing and making jewelry for twenty-five years. It was an accident of fate that led them to kaleido- scopes. A customer asked them to repair a small, damaged brass kaleidoscope. While tack- ling the repair, they did some scope research and tried making a scope of their own. To their surprise, the necklace scopes they created became one of the most popular items at the Sunday art fairs on the beach at Santa Barbara. All of their customers remembered having a kaleidoscope as a child. But even those passers-by who were not familiar with scopes appreciated the tiny, decorative wearable scopes.

Kevin was intrigued with how similar the interior image inside a scope is to the magic circle that is referred to in Hindu as a mandala. "If mandalas produce feelings of inner peace and a sense that life is meaningful, and possesses an order not always perceived," Kevin reasoned, "then surely the scope image is a mandala. So as we embark into this new century, Brewster's *trompe l'oeil* remains a challenge to the artist and viewer alike, to find a place for the magic circle in a ceaselessly changing world."

Wonder-ring. Photo by Ralph Gabriner

Bead-o-scopes. Photo by Allen Bryan

Saturn necklaces surrounding mandala. Photo by Allen Bryan

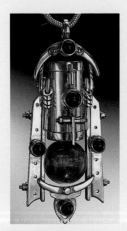

Scope necklace from the
Rocket series.
Photo by Ralph Gabriner

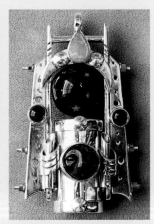

A scope from the **Rocket** series.
Photo by Allen Bryan

Floral **Bead-o-scope**.
Photo by Allen Bryan

Moonbeams necklace.
Photo by Allen Bryan

Saturn necklace.
Photo by Ralph Gabriner

Ann and Shawn Lester

After blazing a new trail in jewelry design, Ann and Shawn Lester converted some of their pieces into wearable kaleidoscopes. They developed an original technique that combines stained or dichroic glass with a hand-pierced silver overlay (even though they were repeatedly told it couldn't be done). Their style was unique when it was invented twenty years ago, and remains so today, partly because of the technical difficulty of enclosing the glass within pierced silver without breaking it with heat or pressure.

Among the few jewelers who do all their own cutting, fabrication, and polishing by hand, Ann and Shawn make each necklace one at a time. Most of them, although tiny, contain two separate mirror systems and are reversible, with a different design on the back and front. Their business, Lightwing Designs, located in a log cabin in the woods of Vermont, reflects their keen interest in the interplay of light, color, translucency, and symmetry. Their jewelry is an attempt to translate the beauty of nature in the form of flowers, birds, and landscapes into silver and glass.

It seems only natural that Ann felt compelled to make their jewelry into scopes when you look at the list of things that fascinate her: optics, geometry, transparency, reflection, mandalas, human perception, beauty, mechanics, motion, shiny colorful objects, and inventions. "The most difficult aspect," she confides, "is learning how to walk when I really want to run and then fly!"

Photo of interior image by Adam Peiperl

Photo of interior image by Adam Peiperl

An assortment of necklace scopes featuring sterling silver with stained and dichroic glass. Many contain two separate mirror systems.
Photos by Allen Bryan

Koji Yamami

Koji Yamami came to the United States in 1983 to study art. While in Los Angeles he saw his first kaleidoscope, and it was love at first sight. When he returned to Japan, he started trying to make kaleidoscopes from memory. His very first scope, in the shape of a large blue dog, won an award. Encouraged by that success, he opened a shop, Little Bear, where he has been selling handmade kaleidoscopes and other glass gifts since 1994, as well as conducting classes on how to make scopes.

After joining the Brewster Society and attending several conventions, Koji and a group of kaleidoscope enthusiasts organized the Japan Kaleidoscope Society. They have also published a book that includes the work of two dozen American artists. While Koji's work is shifting from large to small (one of his most popular styles is a necklace scope), he really wants to build a huge space scope that he can float in!

Although intrigued with the play of light on glass and the way it changes both the exterior and the interior, it is the element of surprise that pleases Koji most. He enjoys the fact that he can never guess what it is really going to look like until he finishes a scope and looks inside. Then every time he gets a fresh surprise. "Kaleidoscopes make every-one happy," Koji says, "and I am happy, too. It was the most important event in my life when I happened to meet kaleidoscopes."

Little Dreams image

Images through tapered mirror systems

Little Dreams necklace

Miniature music box scope

Growing Taller

Each element of the universe, from angels to zodiac signs, vibrates to a particular corresponding color.
Jan Haber designed artistic kaleidoscope patterns for each of the year's astrological signs.

MONTH	BIRTHSTONE	FLOWER
JANUARY	Garnet	Carnation
FEBRUARY	Amethyst	Violet
MARCH	Aquamarine	Jonquil
APRIL	Diamond	Sweet Pea
MAY	Emerald	Lily of the Valley
JUNE	Pearl	Rose
JULY	Ruby	Larkspur
AUGUST	Peridot	Poppy
SEPTEMBER	Sapphire	Aster
OCTOBER	Opal	Calendula
NOVEMBER	Topaz	Chrysanthemum
DECEMBER	Turquoise	Narcissus

ASTROLOGICAL SIGN			GOVERNING ANGEL
Aquarius		January 20–February 18	Gabriel
Pisces		February 19–March 20	Barchiel
Aries		March 21–April 19	Machidiel
Taurus		April 20–May 20	Asmodel
Gemini		May 21–June 20	Ambriel
Cancer		June 21–July 22	Muriel
Leo		July 23–August 22	Verchiel
Virgo		August 23–September 22	Hamaliel
Libra		September 23–October 22	Uriel
Scorpio		October 23–November 21	Barbiel
Sagittarius		November 22–December 21	Adnachiel
Capricorn		December 22–January 19	Hanael

Image through patented mirror system by Don Doak. Photo by Don Doak

7

Oversize, Outdoor, and Beyond

Garden Scope by Robert C. Anderson. Photo by Adam Peiperl

Life unfolds from the center, new beginnings emerge
from the breakup of what came before, all things
turn and spin and change, endlessly rearranging
themselves—the universe is truly a kaleidoscope.

Garden Scope by Robert C. Anderson. Photo by Adam Peiperl

There is good news for those of the school who think "bigger is better," especially for the serious kaleidoscope collector who wants visitors to see scopes from the moment the street number on their mailbox is visible. What more appropriate greeting than Will Smith's "Fountain of Aahs" or Bob Anderson's "Garden Scope"?

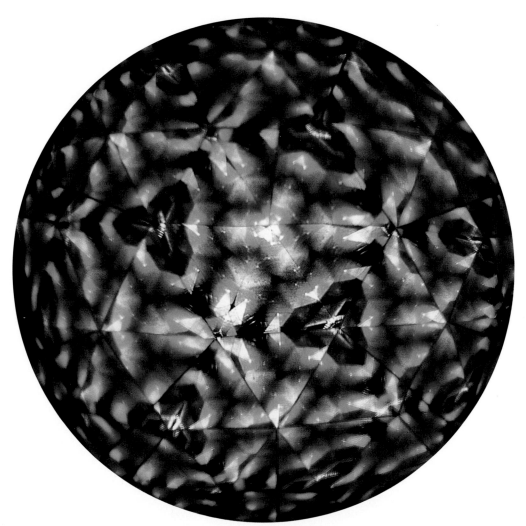

Brewster's Wagon image

Tom Chouteau

Tom Chouteau was the first to specialize in large life-size outdoor kaleidoscopes. Tom possesses a cheerful heart that boosts the spirits of all those around him, as do the large whimsical scopes that are his specialty. "The Kaleidoscope Wagon," Tom's first attempt at an oversized, outdoor scope, was such a big hit that he has continued to develop a whole line of seriously playful kaleidoscopes. His forte is making these scopes out of wood and steel with a lot of strange found objects and recycled parts that most people would consider junk. It is his earnest hope and goal to eventually house all these sculptural creations in an appropriate museum for kids in his hometown of Davenport, Iowa.

When Tom isn't making kaleidoscopes or playing his harmonica, he is busy as a graphic artist for the public library. Reminiscent of his fictional hero, Don Quixote, Tom's fantasy has been to help create a "world wonder." Well, it seems fair to say that he has accomplished just that and by doing exactly what he loves to do most—"build magical kaleidoscopes extraordinaire!"

Two boys view **Dr. Seuss Scope**
Photo courtesy of the Moline Dispatch/Rock Island, Argus, Iowa

Brewster's Peddler Wagon

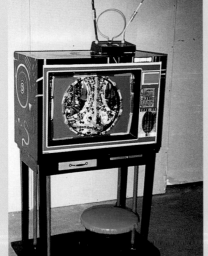

Many Faces TV

The Blue Note

Will Smith

The elements of nature—their greatness, power, and immortality—are the inspiration for many kaleidoscope artists, and never more clearly defined than in the Wave series by Will Smith.

From a small wave necklace and several hand-held "waves" to a floor-model waterfall, Will designs and builds on his basic theme. Even his favorite hobbies—sports, vacations, and daydreaming—involve water: sailing, snorkeling, and warm tropical beaches.

All this is easy to understand when you consider that Will's two college majors were art and oceanography, and that he had created a liquid wave chamber in his late teens which he marketed under the name of "Bottled Oceans." From 1976 to 1993 Will was president of Amazing Plastic Corp., so it was only natural for him to use acrylic as the medium when he decided to put his wave chambers into a line of kaleidoscopes. "Scopes are friends we can count on to nourish us," Will muses. "They provide emotional comfort and inner joy."

Will can be listed among those scope artists who started experimenting on his own, completely unaware that kaleidoscopes had already emerged as a beautiful art form. But with diligence and a personal credo of "you are what you art," he soon made his own waves! Will is confident that beauty exists in everything and everyone, and that learning how to recognize it can become a skill.

Fountain of Aahs
(the waterfall turns the marble object)

Fountain of Aahs image

Wave Scopes. Photo by Adam Peiperl

Detail of **Orbitron**—"where water and waves dance"(pewter)

Steve Failows makes blockbuster scopes—from large burls to virtually the whole tree. Made in the Shade, the name of his business, is a take-off of "Made in America," and "Made in Japan." It also means just hanging out, or fishing in a stream under those trees. But because Steve is able to do what he loves, he says he has it "made in the shade." Born and raised in New York, Steve worked for the U.S. Postal Service before quitting in 1980 to become, in his own words, "a starving artist."

Besides liking his hobbies more than his job, Steve realized he would also prefer to "starve" in warm weather rather than cold, so in 1992 he moved from the Big Apple to Arizona. In addition to making kaleidoscopes (at which point he graduated from "starving artist" to "emerging artist"), Steve enjoys the art of sandblasting glass. "I'm a lucky man," he says, "and I sleep well at night because I'm doing what I want to be doing. I look through a kaleidoscope and it makes me smile. It tickles your brain somewhere."

Green Baroque stained-glass tapered scope on a manzanita burl pedestal

Kaleido-clock

Black iridescent stained-glass tapered scope on a juniper floor stand. Photos by Christopher Marchetti

Bob Anderson

Like so many kaleidoscope artists, Bob Anderson's scope involvement started with collecting. But it was his wife Ann who had been collecting, for several years before they met. In 1994 Bob attended the Brewster Society convention in San Francisco with Ann, and that visit sparked his interest in scopes as an art form. Driven by his passion for metal sculpture, Bob began to think about the possibility of designing an outdoors kaleidoscopic steel sculpture. He envisioned an interactive sculpture that people could display in a deck or garden area.

Because he is both artistic and inventive, Bob studied mirror designs and scope making, and decided that the teleidoscope was his answer. "I loved the concept of an open object chamber. So I designed a heavy-duty brass teleidoscope that was positioned to view a rotating steel bowl. The bowl could be planted with flowers or filled with anything the owner desired. My favorite is fresh flowering plants."

In 1997 Bob began traveling from California to Maine with his Botanica series garden teleidoscopes, exhibiting them at art shows. They were well received everywhere—and not just by kaleidoscope audiences. One of Bob's goals is to introduce scopes into more public places. "It's an opportunity to enrich people's lives on a grand scale," Bob says. "The most exciting moment for me is when someone looks through the scope and a smile immediately lights their face. We share something at that point that transcends all socioeconomic and cultural barriers."

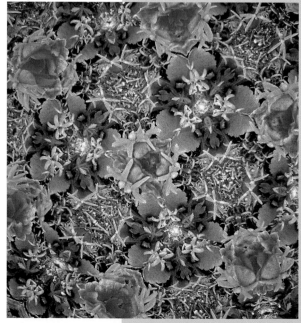

Garden Scope II image

Garden Scope I image

Atomic

Garden Scope II

Sharing Scope

Resourceful and committed are two words that accurately describe Andrew and Robyn Leary. It was an attempt to replace a lost childhood kaleidoscope that prompted the Learys to get into the business of designing and making kaleidoscopes in their native New Zealand. That was about fifteen years ago. Unable to locate the all-important first-surface mirrors required for sharp images, they set out to manufacture their own. This included building the vacuum equipment in which to make the mirrors. They also do all their own brass, acrylic, and wood work, using a native timber that has been recovered from swamps where it has been buried for 40,000 years!

Yet another childhood fascination is incorporated into the kaleidoscopes being made at Scopes New Zealand. Bubbles triggered the idea for a bubble scope. This concept, while great, took a lot of diligent research and hard work. Andrew invented and patented the Ardwen Relay system, which is the integral part of their "Spectrum" and "Black Magic" kaleidoscopes, as well as the key to a host of ideas for future scopes.

On their property in Keri Keri, in addition to a home and studios, there is a little wooden chalet that is perfect for displaying and selling their scopes. They love meeting and greeting people from all over the world who share a love for kaleidoscopes. It is no wonder that Andrew and Robyn consider themselves "the luckiest and busiest Kiwis with the best jobs in the world!"

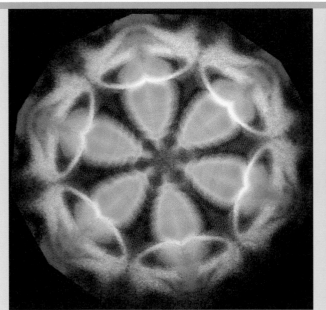

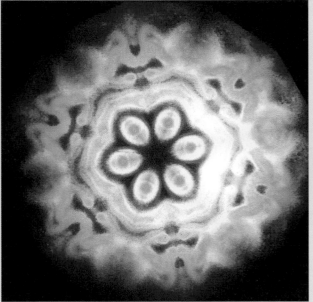

Spectrum Bubble scope images

Spectrum (soap-bubble liquid in object cell forms images). Photo by Gary Landsman

Don Doak

Photo by Bob Vigiletti

The strong light of his mind seems to shine through each kaleidoscope image by Don Doak. Active in the arts and crafts industry for more than thirty-two years, Don has been a self-taught scope maker since 1986. His goal is to spend the rest of his creative years making scopes that explore all the possibilities and variations of his latest patent on specific multiple geometric images.

Don builds all his own tools—including kilns, furnaces, and special heating elements—in his mid-Michigan studio. He has even patented a special magnetically guided glasscutter for making the absolute precise cuts needed to create unique cube and dodecahedron images. Don has made this device available in order to help other artists improve their optics.

In addition to perfecting and patenting geometric mirror systems that create very unusual and complex three-dimensional images, Don also enjoys the kaleidoscope as a tool for relaxation and meditation. "Viewing a kaleido-scope is better than seeing a doctor," he says. "It heals my soul. Perhaps the kaleidoscope's universal appeal is the result of each individual's innate understanding that we, like the shattered, seemingly meaningless pieces of glass in the object cell, fit together perfectly to form a more beautiful picture than any of the parts could ever make alone; that each of us, flawed as we are, is essential and fits perfectly into this large mosaic called humanity."

Image through patented mirror system by Don Doak. Photo by Bob Vigiletti

Images through patented mirror systems by Don Doak. Photos by Don Doak

Marc and Susan Lundgren-Tickle

Marc and Susan Lundgren-Tickle possess an intuitive and almost magical ability to create amazing new dimensions within their kaleidoscopes. They seem to transcend the ordinary, resonating with an amazing color, light, and texture all their own. Most of their designs are derived from the principles of sacred geometry. They use this science to design both the image and the exterior of their scopes, thus preserving an element of continuity to the whole piece.

Marc stumbled into the wonderful world of kaleidoscopes in 1992 when he was asked to proofread a small book on how to make simple kaleidoscopes. As he read it, and then saw a marvelous collection of scopes, it occurred to him that he might be able to make one. "Quite honestly," he relates, "the very next day I had a passion for them, and I could not stop making them. With each one I would try to improve from the last. Since then I have developed a keen interest in the aesthetic combinations and subtle influences of using true geometric principles and pure love of form expressed through creative design."

But the high point for Marc was meeting Susan at a glass studio in North Carolina where he had his studio space. "Shortly thereafter *my work* became *our work*," he says with pride. "She is a joy to be around, and I am so proud of her painting—it is stunning." The adventurous couple moved to Marc's native England and were married there. All the while their experiments with mirrors proved fruitful, and their scopes continue to win praise and awards.

"I am totally convinced that the images that can be created with mirrors, light, and the inclusion of color are infinite," Marc acknowledges. "I genuinely believe that to be true. Every time I go into the studio to experiment, I am so amazed to discover the wonders that can be created. I love it."

Noveau image. Photo by Massimo Strino

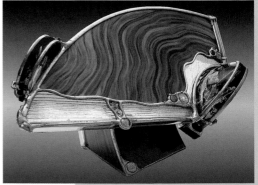

Noveau. Photo by Massimo Strino

Eye of the Soul image

Pacioli image

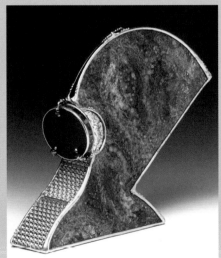

Sir Toby

Eye of the Soul

Avalon

Pacioli

Photos by Ken Pitts

Image and photo by Adam Peiperl

C H A P T E R

Kaleidoscopes and Stress Reduction

Ray Howlett creates light sculptures that virtually explode when viewed through a teleidoscope.

With no predetermined pattern, the sum of its pieces
fit together in an exquisite mosaic of symmetry and balance,
transforming disarray into poetic visions.

Kaleidoscope Viewing Helps Reduce Stress

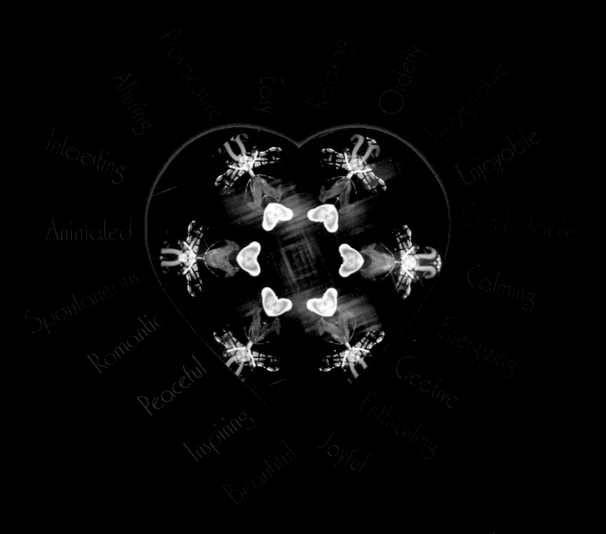

Prismarized image by Randy Knapp. Photo by Adam Peiperl

The kaleidoscope relaxes and energizes at the same time. But whether it is soothing or exhilirating, it generates feelings and emotions that affect our attitudes and actions. The end result of this tempered balance eases anxiety and produces joy and beauty—even in the midst of turmoil or tragedy.

*T*he kaleidoscope does more than entertain, and its positive role goes beyond that of combining art and science in one captivating instrument. Indeed, the kaleidoscope is increasingly recognized for its therapeutic and healing value. It is used in many cancer clinics, hospice groups, and children's hospitals. Nurturing, it seems, ranks next to nutrition for maintaining health and vitality. And according to many, nurturing is also the ultimate function of the kaleidoscope.

Iris Corder

Dr. Hirotomo Ochi, Director of the Institute for Age Control in Fukuroi City, Japan, is more than a casual observer of the healing powers of kaleidoscopes. His research group at the institute conducted numerous experiments that showed the simple act of looking through a kaleidoscope can help lower stress. An "Iris Corder" was used for the experiments, which is a goggles-type piece of equipment with a built-in camera and computer chip that accurately counts how many times the user blinks.

The science of optometry confirms that increased blinking of the eyes is directly proportional to task difficulty, which in turn produces stress. In a relaxed situation, such as kaleidoscope viewing, the number of blinks decreases.

The most noticeable change in the blink rate for both men and women occurred when they viewed the Geo kaleidoscope. Their blink rate decreased to half that during the cognitive task.

But there is more involved in the therapeutic value of the kaleidoscope than eye blinking and reflex time. Sight is the information-collection organ that occupies almost 80 percent of the five senses. Dr. Ochi points out that while sunshine is by far the most beneficial source of light for the human body, people stay inside with artificial lights 90 percent of the time. This adds further stress. He sees the power of the kaleidoscope to relax the body, refresh the soul, and renew the spirit as a very positive means of healing.

Convinced that color is in and of itself healing, Dr. Ochi advises us to know and control colors by studying and selecting those that are suitable and appropriate for our own needs. For this purpose he offers the following color chart that includes suitable foods, along with their corollary effects and conditions.

Know and Control Your Colors

Colors tint our world. They affect our moods, feelings, and looks. A "self-healing power" inherent in colors can influence (both consciously and unconsciously) our actions and reactions. Try to find the color you need, and learn which colors work for you.

NEGATIVE EMOTIONS	COMPATIBLE COLOR	POSITIVE RESULTS	RECOMMENDED FOODS
Despondent, distrustful Despair	White, pink	Refreshed, recharged	Grains, milk, tuna, beans
Insecure, distressed	Blue	Patient, calm	Blueberry, mackerel
Lonely, dejected, anxious	Yellow	Unafraid, comfortable	Banana, lemon, bamboo sprouts, tofu
Impatient, irritable	Orange	Hopeful, confident	Orange, apricot, pumpkin, persimmon
Depressed, stressed	Red	Alert, cheerful	Apple, strawberries, beef, tomatoes
Restless, uneasy	Green	Balanced, healthy	Spinach, parsley, leeks, melon
Fatigued, sad	Purple	Intuitive, positive	Eggplant, red onions, prunes, purple sweet potatoes
Selfish, dissatisfied	Brown	Satisfied, peaceful	Potatoes, chicken, nuts

Hirotomo Ochi, Ph.D.

Mrs. Teruko Tsuji, one of Japan's most revered ceramists, has some of her legendary pieces made into kaleidoscopes.

Dr. Hirotomo Ochi is an accomplished, brilliantly successful businessman who is primarily interested in health and happiness.

Whatever Dr. Ochi sets out to do, he does well, and whatever he aspires to, he achieves. "I can do it! I can do it! Yes, I can surely do it!" This positive affirmation sums up the attitude and spirit of a man who follows his dreams, hopes, and high ideals. The kaleidoscope, he finds, fits perfectly into his business concepts as well as his philosophical outlook. Foreseeing a boom of kaleidoscopes in Japan, Dr. Ochi planned and built the world's first kaleidoscope museum in Sendai, in 1999.

Not content to simply enjoy and display their beauty, Dr. Ochi learned the principles of making kaleidoscopes, and developed some original ideas of his own. His objective is to produce "three-sensory" scopes (combining music and aroma with sight), and to promote them around the world as a tool for healing.

As an inventor and researcher, Dr. Ochi hopes to work with kaleidoscope artists from around the world, using his philosophy of *Kenko-Wado* (a way to appreciate the ideas and rights of others, while sharing values of healthy competition, without fighting). "I find great happiness," he says, "in associating with the many kaleidoscope artists who have pure hearts, and who truly love kaleidoscopes as I do."

Mary, Dave, and Denise Fulkerson, Cozy Baker, and Linda Joy join Dr. Ochi for the opening of the world's first kaleidoscope museum in Sendai, Japan.

Geo image, David Fulkerson designed, built, and installed four GeOchi scopes at the Japan Museum.

Yuriko and Mitsuru Yoda

Yuriko and Mitsuru Yoda incorporate Dr. Ochi's ideas and doctrine in their award-winning kaleidoscopes. They first discovered kaleidoscopes while actively looking for a post-retirement career. They knew immediately this was what they wanted to occupy their lives starting in the new millennium. It fit to perfection their desire to find something that would utilize Mitsuru's engineering skills and Yuriko's dream of creating something beautiful that could at the same time help reduce stress. Their gold-plated electro-motive "Universe 2000" does just that, breaking the aroma barrier as well as that of sound. It resembles the launching pad of a spaceship, about to fly away to the universe to become a light that gives delight and hope to people's hearts.

Yuriko Yoda discovered the healing powers of kaleidoscopes when her younger brother died. She remembers looking into a scope and thinking, "Oh, it's beautiful, and it is a comfort to be able to see beauty even in grief." Her brother had loved scopes, and she lovingly recalls how he used to exclaim "Wow! Wow!" while looking at two different scopes at one time. "If the people in conflict could see a kaleidoscope," he had said, "their feelings may calm down and they might forgive each other."

This tragic event renewed the Yodas' incentive to make original scopes utilizing oriental materials such as bamboo and Japanese lacquer, and reflecting a tenderness that could be an influence for peace and harmony in the world. In their own words, "We want to produce something by hand that is full of dreams, that can make people feel at ease, and convey a message of hope, that there is nothing that is useless in life."

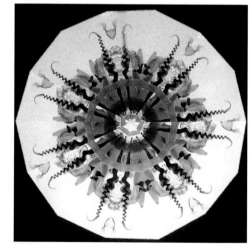
Universe 2000 image

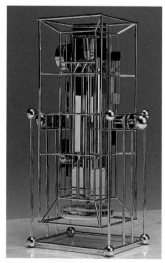
Universe 2000

Japanese Beauty

Bamboo scopes

While one person uses the kaleidoscope as a technicolor tranquilizer, another harnesses its colors to energize. But whether it serves to soothe or stimulate, the interior mandala is the inspiration for diverse renderings by a few artists who do not make kaleidoscopes, but are fascinated with them.

Japanessence. Irene Holler has been painting objects and scenes in repeated segments radiating from the center, which she calls "color scopes," for more than twenty years. At the venerable age of eighty-one, Irene states, "I know from long experience that beauty needs to fill our whole being, and there is no better way to experience beauty than through the moving, dynamic patterns of a kaleidoscope. In the very creating and painting of my color scopes I am able to find an easing from the clutches of sadness and depression. They seem to heal as they continually feed a deep need within."

Kaleidoscope Rose
Lynn Galluzo's "Kaleidographs" are a combination of graphic technology, photography, mirrors, and imagination.

Adam Peiperl combined dancer Alexis Major with his kaleidoscope image via computer manipulation.

Collide-O-Scopic Images is the name Peter Colosi applies "when photography, technology, and art collide to create a beautifully formed image from real things not usually found in a kaleidoscope."

Spider Tree
Gil Krause blends photography, foliage, and collage into a "Pholiage," creating a kaleidoscopic view of the natural world for the mind and spirit.

Jewels in the Air
Betty Tribe transforms the familiar into kaleidoscopic patterns with colored pencil drawings.

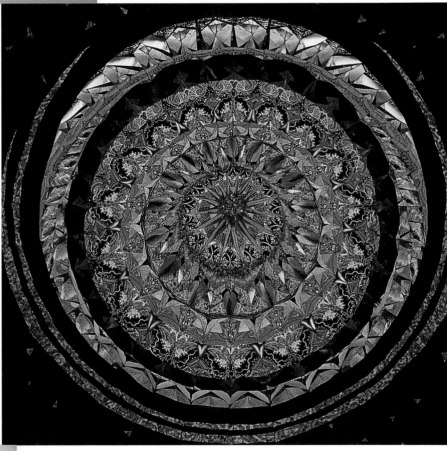

In a New York Minute, 1998.
Paula Nadelstern integrates the idea of a kaleidoscope with the techniques and materials of quiltmaking.
Photo by Karen Bell

Kare O'Neil based her "laid-back realism" in **Kaleidoimage I** on an interior image seen through a Sheryl Koch scope.

Scott Cole has been making kaleidoscopes, and teaching others how to make them, for more than fifteen years. As well as their visual delight, Scott is fascinated with the kaleidoscope's countless metaphors. "Each person creates imagery that is evocative and personal, opening windows that enable us to peer into otherwise hidden realms. As the kaleidoscope offers a reflection of swirling ever-changing events, it adds a perspective that generates beauty and meaning to the random tumble of life. A holistic, transcendent wisdom greater than the pieces, provides a glimpse into the processes of our soul. By seeing ourselves more clearly and discerningly, we are able to recognize the beauty within each of us."

Contact Scott at: Laughing Eye Charlottesville, Virginia (704) 568-4976, email: scott@laughingeye.com

Kay Winkler has been teaching techniques involving stained glass for many years, and making kaleidoscopes for the past twelve years. So conducting kaleidoscope workshops and teaching others to make them came about quite naturally. "It is a real joy to share the procedures and tricks of the trade I have learned over the years," Kay exudes. "I especially love to see the delight of my students when they finish and admire their first kaleidoscope with a turning endpiece. Yes, it's a satisfying and wonderfully rewarding occupation, and I hope to keep on teaching for many years to come."

Contact Kay at:
(302) 299-5176
email: KaleidoKay@aol.com

Marcia Clark feels a divine connection to the kaleidoscope, and after careful reflection, chose Mid-Heaven Creations for the name of her business. "Kaleidoscopes can't take us all the way to heaven," she declares, "but they surely get us part of the way there." To prove the point, Marcia presents a few scopes during her talks, including some beautiful ones that she made herself. She lets the audience view the stress-free imagery, as she expands on the premise that all of life is a kaleidoscope, stressing the clarity, focus, and alignment of our reflecting inner mirror system.

Contact Marcia at: Mid-Heaven Creations Pittsburgh, PA
(724) 941-3228
email: MCPresents@aol.com

The therapeutic benefits that can be derived during the process of viewing kaleidoscope images as well as making them are experienced by a few individuals who share their enthusiasm for scopes with their students.

Where to Find Scopes

ARIZONA
Nellie Bly, Mary Wills, 136 Main St.,
Jerome 86331 (520) 634-0255

Out of Hand, Karen & Bob Klein,
6166 Scottsdale Rd. 82520 (The Borgata),
Scottsdale (602) 998-0977

ARKANSAS
KaleidoKites, Linda & Steve Rogers,
No. IC Spring St., Eureka Springs 72632
(501) 253-6596

CALIFORNIA
Kaleido, Mary Wills, 1001 California Dr.,
Burlington 94010 (650) 558-0864

Eileen Kremen Gallery, 619 N. Harbor
Blvd., Fullerton 92632 (714) 879-1391

Kaleidoscope Gallery, Ed Bolin, 27741
Crown Valley Pkwy. #323, Mission Viejo
92691 (949) 348-0044

The Melting Pot, Skip MacLaren,
Main at Lansing Sts., Mendocino 95460
(707) 937-0173

Moonstones, 1070 Main St., Cambria
93428 (805) 927-3447

Something/Anything, John Woodhull,
900 Northpoint, San Francisco 94109
(415) 441-8003

The Sun Country, Ray & Diane Anderson,
Ocean & San Carlos, Carmel 93921
(408) 625-5907

COLORADO
Human Touch Gallery, Bonnie Willow &
Gary Deetz, 14 Ruxton Ave.,
Manitou Springs 80829 (719) 685-1241

Luma, Cathy Coleman,
The Broadmoor Hotel, Colorado Springs
80906 (719) 577-5835

Millie's Classic Glass, Millie Bloomfield,
127 Douglas St., Sterling 80751
(970) 521-9950

J. Fenton Gallery, 100 Elbert Lane,
Snowmass Village 81615 (970) 923-5457

FLORIDA
Fusion Fine Crafts, John Dallman & Janet
Jones, 118 E. Orange St., Tarpon Springs
34689 (727) 934-9396

GEORGIA
Mole Hole of Atlanta, Steve & Linda
Hyslop, 3500 Peachtree Rd. NE,
Atlanta 30326 (404) 231-4840
The Veranda, Jan & Bobby Boal,
252 Seavy St., Senoia 30276-0177
(770) 599-3905

ILLINOIS
American Hands, Ron Erday,
5311 N. Clark St., Chicago 60640
(773) 728-4227

The Artists' Works, Judy Kaponya,
32 W. Chicago Ave., Naperville 60540
(630) 357-3774

Ginger's, Ginger Lewis, Hotel Baker,
10 W. Main St., St. Charles 60174
(610) 513-8920

Pam's Glass Works, Pam & Tony Orlando,
215 Rob. P. Coffin Rd., Long Grove
60047 (847) 634-6555

IOWA
The Plant Ranch, Karl & Jean Schilling,
507 Highway 65, Manley 50456
(888) 454-2068

KENTUCKY
Artique, Michael Stutland, Civic Center,
410 W. Vine St., Lexington 40507
(859) 233-1774 and 161 Lexington
Green Circle 40503 (859) 272 8802

MAINE
Mack Bear Gallery, George Bear &
Susan Mack, 594 Ocean Point Road,
East Booth Bay 04544(207) 633-7707

MARYLAND
Appalachian Springs, David & Polly Brooks,
1041 Rockville Pike, Rockville 20852
(301) 230-1380

Strathmore Hall Arts Center, Gift Shop,
10701 Rockville Pike, N. Bethesda
20852 (301) 530-0540

MASSACHSETTS
Joie de Vivre, Linda Given, 1791 Mass.
Ave., Cambridge 02140 (617) 864-8188

Whippoorwill Galleries, Karen & Bob Hohler,
126 S. Market, Faneuil Hall, Boston
02109 (617) 523-5149, and Prudential
Center, 800 Boylston St., Boston 02199
(617) 236 2050

Impulse, Sonny Bayer, 188 Commerce
St., Provincetown 02657 (508) 487-1154

MINNESOTA
Davlins, David & Linda Looney,
2652 Southdale Center, 6601 France
Ave. S. Edina 55435 (952) 926-6838,
or 116 Rosedale Center, Rosedale 55113
(651) 631-2162, or The Woods at Maple
Grove 55369 (763) 416-WOOD

The Glass Scope, Charles & Donna Schilling,
314 Main St., Red Wing 55066
(651) 388-2048

MISSOURI
Glass Magic, Mary Bowman, Engler
Block, 1335 W. Hwy 76, Branson 65616
(417) 335-8236

NEVADA
Paper & Gold, Richard Erickson,
Caesar's Tahoe, Stateline (775) 588-4438

NEW JERSEY
Stained Glass Boutique, Lorraine Guglielmi, 79 E. Main St., Chester 07930 (908) 879-7351

Dexterity, Shirley Zafirau, 26 Church St., Montclair 07042 (973) 746-5370

NEW MEXICO
La Casita des Kaleidoscopes, Pat Asay, 206 San Felipe NW #7, Patio Market, Albuquerque 87104 (505) 247-4242

NEW YORK
An American Craftsman, Richard Rothbard, 60 W. 50th St., New York 10011 (212) 307-7161

Enchanted Forest, David Wallace, 85 Mercer St., New York 10012 (212) 925-6677

Glass Menagerie, Dick & Jackie Pope, 37 East Market St., Corning 14830 (607) 962-6300

Hand of the Craftsman, Jan & Shel Haber, 52 Main St., Nyack 10960 (914) 358-6622

Kaatskill Kaleidostore, Dean Gitter, Rt. 28, Mt. Tremper 12457 (914) 688-9700

Craft Company No. 6, Lynn Allinger & Gary Stam, 785 University Ave., Rochester 14607 (716) 473-3413

NORTH CAROLINA
Makado Gallery, Dianna Sprague, 307 N. Front St., Wilmington 28401 (910) 392-7770

New Morning Gallery, John Cram, 7 Boston Way, Asheville 28803 (828) 274-2831

OHIO
27 Queensgate, Richard & Pegi Dickson, 8920 Mentor Ave, Mentor 44060 (440) 974-8600

OREGON
The Bookworm Bookstore, Myrna Barber, 29401 S. Ellensburg, Pacific Coast Hwy 101, Gold Beach 97444 (541) 247-9033

PENNSYLVANIA
Amano, Ana Leyland, 128 S. Main St., New Hope 18938 (215) 862-5122

Celestine Gifts, Sandra Habekost, 254 High St., Pottstown 19464 (610) 970-8050

Mykonos, Barbara Robbins, Glen Eagle Sq., Rt. 202, Chadds Ford 19317 (610) 558-8000

Glass Growers Gallery, Debbie Vahanian, 10 E. 5th, Erie 16501 (814) 453-3758

Chestnut House, Lola & Frank Thomas, 25 W. King St., Lancaster 17603 (717) 393-0111

Wood You Believe, Glenn Straub, The Artworks at Doneckers, 100 N. State St., Studio 126, Ephrata 17522 (717) 738-9595

Heart of the Home, 28 S. Main Street, New Hope 18938 (215) 862-1880

SOUTH CAROLINA
One of a Kind Art & Fine Craft Gallery, Terry & Carlos Gould, 1317 Theater Dr., Mt. Pleasant 29464 (843) 971-1774

TENNESSEE
Hanson Gallery, Doug & Diane Hanson, 5607 Kingston Pike, Knoxville 37919 (865)584-6097

Only Kids, Kathy & Steve Arnold, 6150 Poplar Ave., Knoxville 38119 (865)683-1234

TEXAS
Fleeflight Gallery, Bob Williams, The Shops at Willow Bend, Plano 75093 (214) 521-9422

Nature's Gifts, Rick Cohen, South Plains Mall, 6002 Slide Rd., Lubbock 79414 (806) 791-1265

Through the Looking Glass, Kathy & Charles Esserman, The Shops of River Square Center, 213 Mary St., Waco 76701 (254) 757-0921

Hanson Gallery, Donna & Art Milstein, Galleria II, Level 2, 5085 Westheimer, Houston 77056 (713) 552-1242 and Town & Country Mall 77024-3922 (713) 984-1242

Surprises, Jerry & Liora Cohen, 208 Preston Royal Shopping Village, Dallas, 75230 or 4003 Westheimer, Houston 77027 (713) 877-1900

VERMONT
Stowe Gallery, Stephen Fishman, Mountain Rd., Stowe 05672 (802) 253-4693

The Unicorn (Jeffrey Kahn), 15 Central St., Woodstock 05091 (802) 457-2480

VIRGINIA
Appalachian Springs, David & Polly Brooks, 11877 Market St., Reston 20190 (703) 478-2218

Arts Afire, Joe Egerton, 102 N. Fayette St., Alexandria 22314 (703) 838-9785

Quilts Unlimited, Joan Fenton, 110 S. Henry St., Williamsburg 23185 (757)221-8200; 1051 Millmont, Charlottesville 22903 (434) 979-8110; and Cottage Row, Hot Springs 24445 (540) 839-5955

WASHINGTON, D.C.
Appalachian Springs, David & Polly Brooks, 1415 Wisconsin Ave. 20007 (202)337-5780 and Union Station, 50 Mass. Ave. NE 20002 (202) 682-0505

WISCONSIN
The Red Geranium, Kathy & Walter Vail, Hwy 57, Bailey's Harbor 54202 (920) 839-2360

ENGLAND

The Alexander Collection, Paul & Penny Kustow, No.1, The Broadway, Amersham Old Town, Bucks (01494 434234)

JAPAN

Atelier Rocky Kaleidoscopes Gallery, 1354-7 Yahatano Ito-Shi, Sizuoka-Ken (81-557-55-1755) email: itoh@izu.co.jp

Kaleidoscope Mukashi-kan, Miti Araki, 2-13-8 Azabu, Juban, Minato-ku, Tokyo (+81-3-3453-4415)
email: mukashi-kan@brewster.co.jp and Kaleidoscope Mukashi-kan, Ikspieri, #231, 1-4 Maihama, Urayasu-shi, Chiba-ken (+81-47-305-5802) and Mukashi-kan, Kyoto, Daimaru Kyoto, Shijo-dohri, Shimogyou-ku, Kyoto (+81-75-211-8111)

Seishido Myers Ltd., Fujio Imada, 7-14-8 Roppongi, Minato-ku, Tokyo 106 (+81-3-5459-2005)

Sendai Kaleidoscope Art Museum, Dr. Hirotomo Ochi, 1-2 aza Matsuba Moniwa Taihaku-ku Sendai-shi, Miyaga-ken 982-0251 (+81-22–304-8080)

Little Bear, Koji Yamami, 2-21-19 Denenchofu, Ohta-ku, Tokyo 145-0071 (+81-3-3722-6478)
Vatican, Tomoko Chiba, 4-2-395 Takamori Izumi Sendai 891-32 (+81-22-377-3479)

The Smallest Museum in the World, Shinichi Ohkuma, 7-1-310, Uguisudani-machi, Shibuya-ku, Tokyo 150-0032 (+81-3-3463-6916)

Screen Saver

Many kaleidoscopic screen savers are available, but "Dream Scope" is so satisfying and spectacular that there is no need to list another:
email: dreamscope@nandeska.com
www.nandeska.com/dreamscope

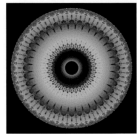 

Index

About the Author

Photo by Gary Landsman

Cozy Baker lives and breathes kaleidoscopes. Her passion for scopes began close to twenty years ago when she discovered one during a search for beauty in the midst of tragedy, following the death of her twenty-one year old son Randall. Since then, kaleidoscopes have literally changed her life, bringing color and purpose to her golden years, which she enjoys with her children and grandchildren in her kaleidoscope house/museum in Bethesda, Maryland.

Cozy has written six books on the subject, owns the world's largest collection, founded The Brewster Society (an international organization for kaleidoscope enthusiasts) and is known and respected by probably every kaleidoscope artist in the country, if not the world. Her efforts in the kaleidoscope field have helped change the market. She has been featured in numerous magazine and newspaper articles, appeared on radio and TV shows, and was named in *Niche Magazine's* list of "20 Who Made a Difference" in the crafts field, among such names as Gustav Stickley, Harvey Littleton, and Lloyd Herman.

From her vantage point at the center of the kaleidoscope world, Cozy provides a revealing insight into the lives of the kaleidoscope artists, who are the very heart of their art.

The Brewster Society

The Brewster Society, named after the inventor of the kaleidoscope, Sir David Brewster, is an international organization for kaleidoscope enthusiasts. Its purpose is to promote and share the beauty, creativity, and joy of these mirrored tubes of magic. It serves as a network for linking kaleidoscope artists, collectors, and retailers. Membership benefits include a quarterly newsletter, an annual convention, regional meetings, and a house/museum, maintained for members and open by appointment only.

One of the missions of the Brewster Society is to donate kaleidoscopes, books, videotapes, financial assistance, and support to various individuals and groups. There is a remarkable camaraderie among the caring and sharing members of this unique organization, and active members agree that the biggest benefit of all is the strong bonding and close friendships that are formed.

Address: PO Box 1073, Bethesda, MD 20817
Phone: (302)365-1855
Fax: (301)365-2284
email: cozybaker1@aol.com
website: www.brewstersociety.com

Also from Cozy Baker and C&T Publishing

For more information write for a free catalog:
C&T Publishing, Inc.
P.O. Box 1456
Lafayette, CA 94549
(800) 284-1114
email: ctinfo@ctpub.com
website: www.ctpub.com